Wiltshire
and Le

G000275257

Farming editor of *The Field* for many years, Ralph Whitlock
has published numerous articles in *The Times*, the *Daily
Telegraph* and other leading journals and writes a regular
column for the *Guardian Weekly*. His frequent radio and
television programmes have included *Cowleaze Farm*,
forerunner of *The Archers*.

Ralph Whitlock is uniquely qualified to write a book
about the folklore of Wiltshire, having lived in the area all
his life and being imbued with a deep understanding of
the land and its legends. He is also the author of more
than a hundred books on the natural history, history and
topography of Britain, including *A Victorian Village*, *The
Lost Village* and *Water Divining*, all published by Robert
Hale. Mr Whitlock lives in Winterslow, near Salisbury.

Wiltshire Folklore and Legends

RALPH WHITLOCK

ROBERT HALE · LONDON

ISBN 0 7090 4740 1

Robert Hale Limited
Clerkenwell House
Clerkenwell Green
London EC1R 0HT

Photoset in Palatino by
Derek Doyle & Associates, Mold, Clwyd.
Printed in Great Britain by
St Edmundsbury Press Ltd, Bury St Edmunds, Suffolk.
Bound by WBC Bookbinders Ltd,
Bridgend, Mid-Glamorgan.

Contents

Acknowledgements

The author would like to acknowledge the help he has derived from the books *Ghosts and Legends of the Wiltshire Countryside* and *Wiltshire Folklore,* by the late Kathleen Wiltshire. Also *The Ghosts of Wiltshire,* by Peter Underwood, and *Weyhill Fair,* by Anthony C. Raper.

1 The Tale of the Wiltshire Moonrakers

The one tale known far and wide to every Wiltshireman is that of the Wiltshire Moonrakers. The story goes that two men from the village of Bishop's Cannings were found raking the surface of a local pond with hayrakes one moonlit night. On being challenged, they pointed to the reflection of the moon in the pond and said they were trying to retrieve 'thik gurt yaller cheese'.

The men who challenged them rode away, laughing, to spread the tale; Bishop's Cannings men, up to their nonsense again. It was too good a story to be confined to Wiltshire, and verses were made up about it. One ballad contained the chorus:

> To zee thik dunder-haided coon
> A-reaking atter the shadder of the moon

And Wiltshire people have been called 'Moonrakers' ever since.

But this tale is, in fact, a subtle compliment. The travellers who accosted the 'Moonrakers' were excisemen, searching for smugglers, and the Bishop's Cannings men had almost been caught with a cartload of contraband brandy. When they had heard hooves approaching and guessed it was the excisemen on their rounds, they tipped their load into the pond. When all seemed clear, they started raking the brandy kegs out of the pond, but the excisemen returned unexpectedly. Pretending to be drunk and feeble-minded was the best trick the smugglers could think of on the spur of the moment. It worked, too. The excisemen had their laugh, but the smugglers kept their brandy.

'The vlies be on the turmuts!' chuckled good Wiltshiremen, quoting the traditional march of the Wiltshire Regiment, 'but there baint no vlies on we!'

There is, however, more to the story than meets the eye. For some reason Bishop's Cannings and, to a lesser extent its neighbour, All Cannings, have attracted an undue share of tall stories. Not vicious ones, but rivalry of a gentler type, of a sort holding the locals up to ridicule. Here is a selection.

1   At one time the people of Bishop's Cannings decided to form a band. Someone remembered there had been a band in the village previously, long ago, and a long and diligent search revealed assorted musical instruments in cottages, outhouses and even in the church vestry. That seemed a convenient place for the band to practise, so the musicians met there weekly until they felt confident enough to appear in public at the village fête. The bandsmen assembled at the vestry and then found, to their consternation, that the doorway had been rebuilt since the time of the previous band and was now too narrow to allow the drum to pass through. So the band marched around the village while the drummer sat, beating time, in the vestry!

2   A dog ran into a garden at Bishop's Cannings and bit the handle of a wheelbarrow, whereupon the gardener sawed off the handle, for fear he should catch rabies!

3   A Bishop's Cannings man notorious for his grumbling went to a farm to buy a hundredweight of potatoes. The farmer, knowing his reputation, allowed him to select his own, so naturally he picked out the biggest ones. Next time he saw the farmer he complained,

'They there big taties were holler in the middle. Thee dost

owe I some more. They holes don't weigh nothing, sno!'

4   A Bishop's Cannings man tried to mend a barrel. It was a difficult job, so he got his small son to sit inside and hold the staves while he hammered. When he had finished and was admiring his handiwork a small voice from inside said,

'Vayther, how be I gwaine to get out?'

And he had to knock out the other end of the barrel to release the boy.

5   Another story concerns the building of the church. The people of the neighbouring parishes noticed two spires were being erected, one bigger than the other. They laughed at the Bishop's Cannings folk for being unable to build two of the same size but were told:

'Ah, we'll soon make the littl'un grow.'

So they piled loads of farmyard manure around the smaller spire. When the heap began to sink they exclaimed,

'There! He be growin' up vine.'

6   Then there is the tale of how almost the entire population turned up in Devizes market-place one evening. Someone in Devizes had told them a comet was due to appear and they had come to town to see it.

Another version, however, is that it was only a carter, his wife and family who came to watch an eclipse of the moon; they brought a rick ladder to place against their waggon, in order to get a better view.

7   The following story of the 'Ticktoad', which was printed in the *Wiltshire Archaeological Magazine*, is another of the Cannings saga:

A shepherd coming home to dinner one day saw on the downs above Cannings a large watch. He had never seen a watch before and, being afraid of the thing, thinking it was something dangerous as he could hear it ticking very loudly, he hurried to the village and told the sexton 'there were a great ugly beast up on the downs, and would he come and see it'.

The sexton was a fat heavy man and said he could not walk that far but persuaded a couple of villagers to wheel him up in a wheelbarrow. Two of them had their spades in their hands and, putting these in the wheelbarrow with the sexton, they made their way up to the spot, guided by the shepherd. On approaching the site they stopped and listened to the loud ticking of the watch.

The sexton said, 'Mates, just wheel I round him,' which was done.

'Now wheel I round him again.'

This was done three times, when the sexton said, 'Mates, chuck I out,' and crawling up nearer the 'beast' and listening for a minute he exclaimed, 'Mates, it be a dangerous ticktoad, so smash en up.'

Whereupon the men with the spades smashed the watch and dug a hole and buried the pieces.

8   Said a Bishop's Cannings man,

'Thesem yer electricity cuts baint run fair. Missus were just cooking me tea when the 'lectricy all went off. But whiles we were sitting there in the dark the bus went by wi' all his lights on!'

What is behind this unusual collection of tales associated with one small parish? There must be something that originally started them off. Looking back over the records of Bishop's Cannings, itself a pleasant but undistinguished village like scores of others in the middle of Wiltshire, we are struck by what John Aubrey, the Wiltshire antiquary, had to say about it, 350 years ago:

Mr Ferraby, the minister of Bishop's Cannings, was an ingenious man, and an excellent musician and made several of his parishioners good musicians, both for vocall and instrumentall musick; they sung the Psalms in consort to the organ, which Mr Ferraby procured to be erected.

When King James the First was in these parts he lay at Sir Edward Baynton's at Bromham. Mr Ferraby then entertained his Majesty at the Bush, in Cotefield, with bucoliques of his own making and composing, of four parts; which were sung by his parishioners, who wore frocks and whippes like carters. Whilst his majesty was thus diverted, the eight bells (of which he was the cause) did ring and the organ played on for state; and after this musical entertainment he entertained his majesty with a football match of his own parishioners. This parish in those days would have challenged all England for musique, foot-ball and ringing. For this entertainment his Majesty made him one of his chaplains in ordinary.

A little later Mr Ferraby and his parishioners, this time dressed in 'shepherds' weeds', were entertaining Queen Anne (King James's queen) with a 'pastorall'.

'A copie of his song,' says Aubrey, 'was printed with a compartment excellently well engraved and designed, with goates, pipes, sheep hooks, cornucopies, etc....'

Well, any proper Wiltshire neighbour, seeing this lot, would feel the urge to take the Bishop's Cannings people down a peg or two, lest all the glory should go to their head. And the habit still lingers. When someone thought up the story of the unfair electricity cuts, what more natural than to attach it to Bishop's Cannings.

2 The Stones

Traditions and legends connected with sites such as Stonehenge and Avebury are of two types. We can differentiate, or at least attempt to differentiate, between what local people say and what early scholars have written. In the case of Stonehenge, it is likely that some of the local oral legends derive in part from written records.

In the official guide-book to Stonehenge Professor R.J.C. Atkinson writes: 'Stonehenge is unique. There is nothing like it anywhere else, and from the earliest times it has aroused the awe and curiosity of its visitors.' He is probably right, but the awe did not extend to local folk. They seem to have simply regarded Stonehenge as part of the scenery. I was born within ten miles of the site, and my father in his early days as a shepherd followed his sheep on the neighbouring downs long before barbed-wire or motor traffic existed. We heard only one Stonehenge legend, which I will shortly tell. I remember being taken there to picnic as a small boy, in our first car during the early 1920s. We sat on the stones and played around them. There was no one else in sight, on all the vast grassy plain. It was a pleasant place to visit, with nothing awesome or sinister about it. I remember hundreds of rabbits scampering over the close-cropped turf.

The local attitude towards the 'hanging stones' is probably typified by the activities of 'Gaffer Hunt of Ambresbury', recorded by Dr John Smith, an eighteenth-century worthy who wrote a highly imaginative book about Stonehenge while staying at Boscombe following an inoculation against smallpox.

'Gaffer Hunt', says Dr Smith, 'built a hut against the upright stone of Mars; and attended there daily with liquors, to entertain the traveller, and show him the stones. His cellar was under the great stone next the hut.'

It is a homely and realistic touch among all the fancies about King Bladud, Boadicea, the Hyperboreans, Divitiacus, the Druids, the Formorians and other characters real and imaginary known to antiquity. Gaffer Hunt, showing off the stones to travellers, may well have told them the only oral legend I have heard from residents in villages nearby. This is what it says:

Stonehenge was built by the devil in a single night. He flew back and forth between Ireland and Salisbury Plain, carrying the stones one by one and setting them in place. As he worked he chuckled to himself, imagining the surprise of the local inhabitants when they awoke next morning and saw what had happened.

'That'll have 'em puzzled!' he boasted. 'They'll never know how the stones came there!'

But a friar was lurking in a ditch nearby, watching all. When he heard the devil's boast he couldn't resist exclaiming, in broad Wiltshire,

'Ah! That's more than thee ca'st tell!'

The devil, startled, dropped the stone he was carrying into Bulford Brook, where it can still be seen, immovable. In his anger he picked up one of the largest stones he could find and hurled it at the friar, who was, naturally, running away. So the stone only struck his heel, and the mark it made can still be seen today, on the Heel Stone which stands isolated from the main structure, by the edge of the road.

The friar, and indeed the story as a whole, suggests the Middle Ages. The stones are the work of the devil, and the friar, representing the Christian Church, gets the better of him; this implies a recognition of the site as in some way hostile to the new religion.

Another interesting detail is that the stones were said to come from Ireland. Most of them, the sarsens, were almost certainly fetched from the Marlborough Downs but some, the so-called 'blue stones' came from farther afield. The nearest place to Stonehenge where this type of stone is found is the Prescelly Mountains, in Pembrokeshire; hence it is generally assumed that that was their source. It is interesting, though, that the direction indicated is south-west – the same direction as Ireland.

It is by no means certain that the story of the devil and the friar is an authentic piece of orally transmitted folklore. For we find what seems to be the germ of the story in the *Histories of the Kings of Britain*, written down by that highly imaginative romancer, Geoffrey of Monmouth, in the twelfth century.

Geoffrey begins by quoting, with liberal embellishments of his own, a tale evidently read in the chronicles of a ninth-century writer, Nennius. It concerns Vortigern, king of Britain in the years after the departure of the Roman armies, and Hengist, one of the early leaders of the Saxon invaders. Hengist persuaded the British nobles to attend a peace conference, unarmed, and then treacherously massacred them all. Geoffrey offers the additional information that the massacre occurred at Sarum, 'on the calends of May', and that the number of 'earls and princes' who had their throats cut was 460.

After the ineffectual Vortigern had disappeared from the scene, he was succeeded by a stronger leader, Ambrosius Aurelianus, who is supposed to have given his name to Amesbury. One day at Sarum Ambrosius remembered the nobles who had fallen and 'was moved to pity and tears began to flow. At last he fell to pondering ... in what wise he might best make the place memorable, the green turf that covered so many noble warriors'.

Now Merlin, the Celtic magician who figures so

prominently in the legends of Arthur, appears and makes a speech:

> If thou be fain to grace the burial-place of these men with a work that shall endure for ever, send for the Dance of the Giants that is in Killaurus, a mountain in Ireland. For a structure of stones is there that none of his age could raise save his wit were strong enough to carry his art. For the stones be big, nor is there stone anywhere without virtue. And so they be set round this plot in a circle, even as they now be set up, here shall they stand for ever.

The king burst out laughing and said, 'How may this be, that stones of such bigness and in a country so far away be brought thither, as if Britain were lacking in stones enough for the job.'

Merlin answered, 'Laugh not so lightly. In these stones is a mystery ... and a healing virtue against many ailments. Giants of old did carry them from the furthest ends of Africa and did set them up in Ireland what time they did inhabit there. Not a stone is there that lacketh in virtue of witchcraft.'

Convinced, Ambrosius sent an expedition to fetch the stones. He was opposed by the Irish king, Gilloman, whom he quickly defeated. Transporting the stones, however, proved a more formidable task. Merlin watched the army using 'hawsers, ropes and scaling ladders' without success, and he 'burst out laughing. He put together his own engines, laid the stones down as lightly as none would believe, and bade them carry them to the ships. They returned to Britain with joy and set them up about the compass of the burial-ground in such wise as they had stood on Mount Killaurus ... and proved once again how skill surpasseth strength.'

The Merlin of folklore seems to have had his origin with Geoffrey of Monmouth, and, if at some stage, there is confusion between the magician and the devil, it could account for points of resemblance between Geoffrey's story and the one I heard from Wiltshire countrymen earlier this century. The period is, of course, entirely wrong, but the suggestion of the legendary value attached to the stones is interesting. And I am intrigued by the insistence that Merlin transported the stones, not by magic nor by tucking them under his arm and taking flight, but by specially constructed 'engines', which conveyed them to the ships. This last detail, however, was soon lost, and when in the early years of the seventeenth century Michael Drayton published his *Polyolbion* he had returned to the version in which Merlin brings the stones from Ireland in a single night 'by his skill and magic's wondrous might.'

So we are left with the query, 'Which came first, the written tale as recounted by Geoffrey of Monmouth or the oral tradition current among local people earlier in this century?' Did Geoffrey tap local sources in his day, or had someone who had read Geoffrey retold his story to people in the villages around Stonehenge? Or, as some suggest, did Geoffrey make it all up? Who can say?

I have never been able to find in local folklore any evidence for the association of Druids with Stonehenge. The idea was popularized by the Wiltshire antiquary, John Aubrey, who was born in 1627, and blossomed into increasingly wild theories until we have the stones being assigned to the Phoenicians, the inhabitants of legendary Atlantis and, finally, to a tribe of North American Indians.

In 1781 'The Most Ancient Order of Druids' was founded in London. To this group belong the white-robed dignitaries who, when not disrupted by hooligans, assemble at Stonehenge for mystic rites at dawn on the Midsummer Solstice. These modern Druids are accepted by some as a genuine part of legendary Stonehenge, but there seems to be no valid evidence for any connection between their rituals and beliefs and those of the Druids of pre-Christian Britain.

The authentic Druids were an order of priests, magicians, and medicine-men who apparently established themselves in the Celtic lands of western Europe in the centuries following 500 BC. They were suppressed in Gaul by Julius Caesar and in Britain soon after the Roman conquest, though their influence lingered long afterwards. We have no real knowledge of their beliefs and activities; nearly all the meagre information at our disposal was filtered through hostile sources, such as Roman adversaries and monastic scribes. Some writers believe the Druids were a priesthood of advanced thinkers, possessed of much scientific knowledge and motivated by a belief in one God. Others regard them as medicine-men who practised human sacrifice and even cannibalism. Perhaps the truth lies somewhere between these two extremes.

Stonehenge was built, in several stages, between 1800 and 1400 BC. Did the Druids on their arrival in Britain take over the 1,000-year-old sacred site and use it for their own purposes, as missionaries of other new religions have done with sacred sites in many parts of the world? We search in vain for evidence.

Avebury also tempted antiquaries of the seventeenth, eighteenth and nineteenth centuries to effusions resembling those about Stonehenge but with even more meagre evidence. Avebury was apparently erected in two stages between 1700 and 1500 BC. The great circle, surrounded by ditches and banks, is spacious enough to hold the major part of the modern village of Avebury. Within it were once two smaller circles, and a third may have filled the space now occupied by the northern entrance. Around the inner edge of the encircling ditch were perched about a hundred huge stones, the heaviest weighing over 40 tons. Although not dressed, they seem to have been selected for their shape. Stones with vertical sides and others lozenge-shaped stand alternately. They are typical of the sarsen stones still to be found lying on the Marlborough Downs.

There is little oral lore connected with the stone circle of

Avebury. The chief local tradition concerns the technique for smashing the stones!

John Aubrey describes it in his *Natural History of Wiltshire*: 'They make a fire of that line of the stone where they would have it to crack; and, after the stone is well heated, draw over a line with cold water, and immediately give it a smart knock with a smyth's sledge, and it will break like the collets at the glass-house.'

John Britton, who edited and commented on the 1847 edition of Aubrey's work, remarks: 'This system of destruction is still adopted on the downs in the neighbourhood of Avebury. Many of the upright stones of the great Celtic temple in that parish have been thus destroyed in my time.'

From a south-eastern point on the perimeter of Avebury circle a winding avenue, marked by similar though smaller stones, leads to the crest of Overton Hill, about two miles away. It is recorded that a stone circle stood here until early in the nineteenth century. Archaeologists at present think that it may be older, by a few centuries, than the stone circle of Avebury.

Early antiquarians, like William Stukeley, fancied that the whole complex was a centre for serpent worship. Avebury itself, he thought, represented the coiled body of the serpent, its neck extending along the Kennet avenue to the top of Overton Hill and the stone circle forming its head. A second winding avenue leading south-westwards to Beckhampton, where a few stones are standing, was supposed to be the serpent's tail. Modern authorities, however, do not accept this explanation.

Just over a mile south of Avebury, between the River Kennet and the modern main road, is Silbury Hill. Guide-books usually describe it as the largest artificial hill in Europe. Covering five acres and standing 130 feet high, it is built of chalk rubble from a nearby ditch. Once again, the devil is said to have built the monument in a single night, carrying the earth and chalk in a sack on his back.

According to another version, it is the burial mound of a king named Sil, or, in Wiltshire dialect, Zel. He was buried there erect, on horseback, and the whole task of raising the mound was completed 'while a posset of milk was seething'. As a matter of fact, its making involved moving 670,000 tons of chalk, a task which required an estimated 18 million hours of work by men using antler picks. And a long series of excavations, culminating in one of many months in 1968 and 1969 in full view of the BBC cameras, revealed nothing.

In a book entitled *The Silbury Treasure*, the author, Michael Danes, claims that he knows the answer to the enigma. The hill itself, he believes, is the Mother Goddess of an old religion.

Our ancestors believed that the essential function of a woman was to give birth, so it seemed sensible to them to depict the goddess as a heavily pregnant woman about to give birth. And that, says Mr Danes, is exactly what Silbury is; a huge, three-dimensional goddess in a squatting position. Her form is outlined by the water which surrounds the hill. If, at the appropriate time, you stand on the terrace which surrounds the top of the hill you can witness the birth of the child which the goddess is bearing!

The sequence of events is as follows. At 7.35 p.m. the sun sets. At 8 p.m. the moon rises. The moon is the 'baby'. After its 'birth' at 8 o'clock you can see it in various positions with relation to its mother, such as lying on her knee, until at ten minutes past midnight it reaches its maximum altitude. That, according to Mr Danes, was the moment for cutting the umbilical cord and probably for the ceremonial cutting of the first stalks of corn, which he thinks were probably growing in a sacred patch on the top of the hill. It was, in fact, the signal for the beginning of harvest.

And when was this all-important date? Why, Lammas-tide, of course. Nowadays Lammas falls on 8 August, but to fit in with the less precise calendar of primitive man a margin of a week or two has to be allowed. The key factor is that the festival was observed when the full moon rose within half an hour or so of sunset. And that occurs approximately midway between midsummer and the autumnal equinox.

I am assured that it is still possible to stand on the top of Silbury at the rising of the Lammas-tide full moon and to watch the Earth Mother giving birth to the moon, as she did to the satisfaction of those neolithic people who shifted all those tons of chalk and soil in her honour, nearly five thousand years ago.

According to local tradition, King Zel, notwithstanding the evidence against his existence, may sometimes be seen on moonlit nights, riding around the hill dressed in golden armour. A headless man is also said to have been seen. In the eighteenth and early nineteenth centuries Palm Sunday was the occasion a procession of Avebury villagers made their way to the top of Silbury, there to 'eat fig cakes and drink sugar and water'. Records describe the hill as being crowded with people on Palm Sunday afternoons.

On one occasion during World War I Miss Edith Olivier was surprised to see lights moving among the Avebury stones at night. She also heard gay music, of the kind associated with fairs and assumed that one was being held there. Enquiries revealed that such a fair used to be held within the stone circle at Avebury, though it had been discontinued more than fifty years earlier. A teacher at Lackham School of Agriculture, passing Avebury one moonlight night not many years ago, was startled to see small figures moving among the stones.

In 1938 the skeleton of a man was found by excavators under one of the big stones of Avebury; it had evidently fallen on top of him. From the scissors he carried in his belt it seemed that he was a tailor; silver coins in his pouch dated his death at approximately 1320. It is assumed that he was helping with a stone-smashing operation when the boulder toppled over and crushed him, though there is no local tradition about him.

On the other side of the River Kennet is a spectacular prehistoric tomb, West Kennet Long Barrow. Probably built in about 2000 BC, which makes it older than Avebury and Stonehenge, it was evidently used as a kind of family vault for several centuries. Associated with it is the ghost of a man said to have been a priest. He has been seen entering the barrow at sunrise on the longest day, accompanied by a big white dog with red ears, the traditional fairy colouring.

Woodhenge, which can be termed a timber counterpart of Stonehenge and which stood about two miles north-east of it, was discovered by air photography in the 1920s. It stands just outside an enormous prehistoric circle of which virtually nothing is known. M.E.Cunningham, in her *Introduction to the Archaeology of Wiltshire*, records that one of the most striking features of Woodhenge is the burial 'in a grave occupying the same relative position to the rings that the "altar" stone does to the circles of Stonehenge. The burial is that of a young child, about three years of age, whose skull had been cleft before burial, thus suggesting that the burial was in the nature of a dedicatory or sacrificial one'.

The Wiltshire Downs, particularly Salisbury Plain, contain one of the largest concentrations of barrows in Europe. In some of those which have been excavated treasure has been found – objects of gold, copper, bronze and amber. Although a number of these barrows were opened by local people before professional archaeologists became interested in them, few have legends attached to them. But they were sometimes linked with the devil, as in the Devil's Den, or with giants, as in the Giant's Grave.

The Devil's Den, however, a megalithic grave near Marlborough, is haunted by a dog, 'with huge, burning eyes'. It is white and apparently has its kennel underneath the tomb. Sometimes at night the devil can be seen trying to shift the stones with the help of four white oxen. Doghill Barrow, near Stonehenge, also has a ghostly dog. A barrow on Roundway Down, near Devizes, was haunted by a human ghost which led people to it. Since 1855, when the barrow was excavated, the ghost has not been seen.

Manton Barrow, near Marlborough, which was excavated in 1906, contained the body of an old woman adorned with ornaments of gold, amber, bronze and lignite. Nearby was a cottage occupied by a widow whose husband had been employed by a Dr J.B.Maurice of Marlborough. After the excavation and the reinterment of the skeleton, the barrow was made up and planted with trees. The widow told Dr Maurice that 'every night since that man from Devizes came and disturbed the old creature she did come out of the mound and walk around the house and squinny into the window. I do hear her most nights and want you to give me summat to keep her away.' The doctor gave her some medicine, telling her to go to bed in the dark immediately after taking it. Later the widow said, 'The old creature came round the cottage as usual for a few nights but, not seeing me, gave up, thinking no doubt she had scared me away.'

3 The Highway

The link connecting all the following mysterious events is that they all happened on or near a highway. One of the most convincing befell Mrs Edna Hedges on a warm, sunny afternoon in the early 1930s when, as a girl in her early teens, she went to pay a visit to a best friend who had recently moved to another village. She was busy with the tales she intended to relate at their meeting and so failed to notice a thunderstorm brewing until it was nearly upon her.

The road was a lonely one and, in the early 1930s, carried little traffic. There was no shelter in sight except for a thatched cottage with a little smoke coming from the chimney, standing alone a little way down a side lane. So she hurried down the lane, just as the storm was breaking, and knocked at the door.

It was opened noiselessly by an old man, who stood looking at her questioningly. When she explained her need he showed her where to park her bicycle and beckoned her inside. He was tall, with broad shoulders, long grey hair and beard and an old-fashioned pipe in his mouth. She remembered he wore a dark green waistcoat with metal buttons. The room was dark and low-ceilinged, with a bright fire burning in an old-fashioned grate. He looked at her and smiled, but afterwards she realized that he had never spoken to her.

Nor did she have any recollection of leaving the cottage; only that the storm was over and she was well on her way.

When she arrived there were other visitors at her friend's house for tea. The cottage was off the road from Stratton St Margaret to Wanborough – an old Roman road – and one of the visitors remarked, 'If you cycled from Hannington you must have been caught in it.'

'But you were quite dry when you arrived,' said her best friend. So the story of the shelter in the cottage was told, and at once there was a chorus of, 'Oh but there isn't a cottage on all that stretch of road ...' until one person recalled, 'Only that derelict one which no one has lived in for these fifty years!'

It was almost dark when Mrs Hedges returned home and she had no chance of visiting the cottage again for several weeks. When she did so she found it completely derelict. The cottage was certainly there, but half the thatch had caved in. Rafters were exposed to the sky, the door hung askew on its hinges, and the broken window-panes were green and murky. What had once been a garden was a jungle, and the smell of decay was everywhere.

Mrs Hedges was often questioned about her experience but always stuck to her story. She can never explain it, but it really did happen!

At Shockerwick Bridge a phantom car suddenly appears when you are driving to or from Bath at midnight. It appears from nowhere ... and the car you are in drives straight through it! The car is said to be an old-fashioned, blunt-nosed, blue Morris Minor.

In 1921 or 1922 a Mr Tilley was cycling along the stretch of road between Seend fork and the Seend sawmills when he saw the approaching service bus coming from Maple Hill, with all the internal lights on. As he approached the Seend fork he glanced to the hill on his right, to see what traffic was coming from that direction – and in that split second the bus disappeared! He rode on, expecting to meet up with it and thinking that it had stopped with some trouble, but he never set eyes on it again.

A lady was driving her car near Pickwick, Corsham, when she was passed by a large American-style car with its lights full on. She allowed it to pass her up the hill – and then realized that it had no driver!

A reporter on the *Marlborough Times*, travelling from his home at Ogbourne St Andrew each day, noticed that at a certain spot on his journey he always felt very cold, regardless of the weather. He also confessed to feeling a 'presence' inside the car. On one occasion, glancing into the driving-mirror, he saw a 'grey shape' in the back of the car. At a certain spot it left the car, and the temperature returned to normal. He asked his girlfriend to accompany him, and together they fixed up a second mirror for her. At the very spot where the man had had his uncanny experience the girl exclaimed, 'Is this the place?' She too could see the 'grey shape'!

At about 7 p.m. one winter evening Mr Burcombe, a taxi-driver of Bath, was driving along the Bath to Melksham road, near Atworth, when something came out of the hedge on one side of the road and crossed in the beam of his headlights. Mr Burcombe had to jam on his brakes to avoid a collision, apparently with a man on horseback. Stopping to investigate, he was surprised to find no opening on either side of the road that would admit the passage of a horseman. He was accompanied by Mrs Burcombe, who witnessed the incident.

And then there was Mrs Kennedy, of Great Bedwyn, who on a dull wet night thought she picked up a ghost on the Great Bedwyn to Newbury road. She was on her way to Newbury to pick her daughter up from a class there when she passed a person dressed in what she took to be a white mackintosh standing by the roadside. Immediately afterwards she suddenly felt very cold and had the feeling that someone had got into the car and was sitting behind her. When she reached Newbury the ice-cold air seemed to disappear, and when her daughter got into the car she remarked on how beautifully warm it was.

Mrs Kennedy still maintains that she gave a ghost a lift that night, in spite of her husband's theory that what she saw was an optical illusion, created by raindrops.

Two young men were returning from Swindon to Broad Blunsdon at about two o'clock one morning, having been attending a bowling match, when suddenly, at a spot known as the Fork-ed Elm, they saw an odd figure by the roadside. It had long, untidy hair and was dressed in white. They couldn't tell whether it was male or female but the odd thing about it was that its feet were about a foot above the grass at the edge of the road! They were too astonished to stop immediately, but, having gone a little distance down the road and having told each other what they had seen, they turned the car round and went back. They found nothing.

Next day one of the young men and his father went to examine the spot and found no sign of anything at all – no footprints, no grass trampled, no hedges broken – nothing!

In the village of Bulford a woman is said to emerge from the gates of a big house, cross the road and then go straight through a wire fence on the opposite side. A lorry driver who saw her pulled up suddenly as he thought he had hit her. Looking back he saw her go straight through the barbed-wire fence and disappear. Kathleen Wiltshire, who describes the incident, says he arrived at his destination very much shaken!

And in 1936 a man driving to meet his wife from a New Year's party at Potterne gave a lift to a young woman, dressed in a green suit with a dark collar, who was waiting at the roadside. When she got into the back of the car the air grew suddenly cold. He glanced back, and there was no one there. She had completely vanished.

A strange encounter occurred at Allington, where the Horton road skirts the foot of Tan Hill. It happened on the last Sunday in October, the 30th, in 1904 to a Mr Alfred Fielding, who was a Methodist local preacher for seventy years, though on this occasion he was a young man of 24. He and another preacher were driving home from service in a horse and trap, when a heavy storm blew up. Through the pouring rain they saw the figure of a woman in white approaching them. The horse stopped dead, and as they watched the girl advancing one of them remarked to the other what a pity it was for her to be out on such a night, and in such a nice white dress. As she drew level with the lights of the trap they saw she had a most attractive and indeed angelic face and auburn hair. Then she vanished. The men called to her, but there was no response.

Mr Fielding commented, 'Up to then I had never believed in ghosts, thinking them mere "women's tales".'

In about 1880 a Mr and Mrs Plank were going home by pony and trap from West Lavington to New Zealand Farm on Imber Down. They had been doing their week-end shopping at Lavington and on this occasion they missed their way in a fog. Not being sure where they were they stopped and were debating which way to go when a white-robed figure passed them. They both saw it, and even the pony saw it, for he pricked up his ears! But there was no logical explanation.

Similarly, many years ago, a lady when out hunting saw a market woman, dressed in old-fashioned clothes, at the top of a hill near Bremhill, near Maud Heath's monument. The horse was terrified and required all its rider's attention to quieten it. When the lady had leisure to look again the old woman had disappeared, nor was there any convenient way, such as a field gate, by which she could have gone!

In 1921 or 1922 Mr T.W.Tilley, already mentioned, was cycling from Melksham to Poulshot and back three evenings a week. One night, at about 10.30, he had just reached the Poulshot turning on his homeward journey, when someone started to whistle to him from the top of the bridge. Then someone began to call him, 'Come up here! Come up here!' He hesitated but did not stop.

Two mornings later the body of a man, whom Mr Tilley recognized, was found on the grass verge beneath a high wall at the side of the bridge. An inquest was held and brought in an open verdict. Mr Tilley comments that his mother always swore that that would have been his fate if he had answered that call.

And here is a more recent episode. A Mr H.Tyrell, aged 64, was taking his usual way to work at RAF Hullavington and had turned his car right at the main road. It was exactly 6 a.m., and the headlights were not full on. Suddenly he saw the figure of a man walking in the middle of the road and, although he was not driving quickly, he tried to pull up. But he seemed unable to do so. The man seemed to be dressed in grey overalls, with a bright buckle at the waist. He was a sharp-featured man aged about 40 and had a very white face. He turned sideways towards the verge, raised his arm – and vanished!

'I have thought about it a lot since,' says Mr Tyrell, 'and although I can hardly believe it, the only explanation is that I have seen a ghost!'

At the spot where this incident occurred there was once a pond, known as Horse Pool, but since filled in. There is a story that many years ago a coach and horses were driven into the pond and all the passengers were drowned.

A motorist was driving his car one night along the road to Allington, near All Cannings, and had just passed Woodborough station when he saw coming towards him a man dressed as a cavalier, with feathered hat, lace collar, satin doublet and breeches, and wearing a rapier. The motorist at first thought he was encountering a man in fancy dress but then noticed that the man was leading a huge black hound on a lead. And the eyes of the dog did not reflect the car lights, as an animal's eyes usually do!

When recounting the tale to his wife she asked him at this stage of the narrative, 'What did you do then?'

He shuddered. 'I put my foot down and drove like hell!'

In 1957 a Mr Sidney Martin was teaching his wife, Lilia, to drive a car on the Hungerford/Salisbury road when they both saw a lovely lady riding on a white horse. She crossed the road at right angles in front of them, apparently following an ancient right-of-way. They watched her until a bend in the road hid her from view.

On making enquiries they found that the local people did not know her name but had frequently seen her and referred to her as 'the lovely lady on horseback'. The postman said he had often seen her when on his rounds.

As recently as 1972 several residents of Bishop's Cannings had seen the Pond House ghost. He is said to be a 'little old man', dressed in old-fashioned clothes. He walks along the field path from an old thatched house in the hamlet of Coate to another old thatched house, known as Pond House, crossing a bridge on the way. Pond House has the reputation of being haunted, with strange bumps and noises at times and an icy air being felt. But the family who lived in the Pond House for many years have no idea who the old man may be.

Whether it is this old man or another, a figure of a man carrying a pack on his back is often seen walking at dusk along a lane at the back of Bishop's Cannings church. One young man heard the footsteps of this apparition behind him and overtaking him. Curious, the young man quickened his own pace when, suddenly, what he described as a 'huge tail' shot out and struck him in the face, almost blinding him. When he recovered from the shock, he was alone on the road.

And now here are some 'shorts', meaning spectral occurrences about which nothing is known except that they have been reported.

On Granham Hill, near Marlborough, a coach is said to be driven, on the stroke of midnight, through a gap in a hedge, by a headless coachman!

At Chalk Pit Hill, near Amesbury, when conditions are right one can hear the sounds of a coach approaching and then receding in the distance.

At Whetham Bottom, near Calne, a carriage drawn by six grey horses is said to have been seen by 'lots of folk'.

On Christmas Eve a coach and four cross a bridge at Vorty Green, near Calcutt, Cricklade.

A headless horse can be seen galloping along Church Lane, Crockerton.

On Salisbury Plain, where the Lavington road branches off the main Devizes road, a colour sergeant murdered a drummer-boy for his pay in the 1770s. Some years later when revisiting the scene he thought he saw the apparition of the drummer-boy and heard him drumming. He was so frightened that he broke down and confessed to the murder. He was hanged at Devizes.

The ghost of William Boulter, the Wiltshire highwayman hanged in 1778 still rides on Salisbury Plain on dark and stormy nights, especially on stretches of the A30 road.

A woman in black walks along the Roman road between Mildenhall and Wilton. She has been taken for a living woman but walks so fast that no one can catch up with her.

The following letter from Sir Michael W.S.Bruce was printed in the *Evening Standard* on 23 December 1953:

Shortly before D-Day I was sent on a course of instruction to Larkhill. Four of us went with an RAF/WO in a jeep to select suitable gun-sites; we were coming up from the north towards the road which runs past Stonehenge, and between us and the road lay a small copse; suddenly we all saw a very small aircraft dive straight down into the wood and disappear into the wood and disappear in the trees; we raced the jeep up to give assistance; there was no sign of a crash – nothing – nothing flying away to the south. Suddenly I heard the WO shout; he was standing white-faced before a large stone cairn commemorating the first death from an aeroplane accident in this country in 1912. It has been suggested that the apparition was that of Colonel F.S.Cody, pioneer of military aviation, who died nearby in his experimental aircraft. His was actually the first death in powered heavier-than-air flight; but the monument refers to Captain B.Loraine and S/Sergeant R.Wilson, who died in 1912, the first members of the RFC to do so.

Twice in its career The Pheasant Inn (Winterslow Hutt) has achieved national celebrity, once in 1816 when the incident of the lioness occurred and once in 1989 when it featured on a postage stamp issued to mark the centenary of the Royal Mail.

The facts of the story are these. On an October night in 1816 the Exeter mail-coach, *en route* for London, stopped at the inn as usual when one of the leading horses was pounced upon by a lioness! The coachman thought at first that the assailant was a calf but was soon enlightened. The animal belonged to a travelling menagerie which was putting up there for the night, and no one knew it had escaped until it indulged in this piece of unprovoked aggression. And then what a buzz there was!

The horse, an ex-racehorse named Pomegranate, put up a spirited defence but became entangled in the traces and nearly overturned the coach. The passengers tumbled out of the coach and rushed into the inn, bolting the door. The mail guard drew his blunderbuss but was threatened with a pistol by the menagerie proprietor, who was unwilling to lose such a valuable animal. He called up his dog, said by one account to have been a Newfoundland and by another to have been the menagerie's mastiff, who seized the lioness by the hind leg and promptly suffered the consequences. The lioness, now as alarmed as everyone else, took refuge under a granary, where she crouched among the staddle-stones.

What followed, as reported in the *Salisbury & Winchester Journal* in the following week, strikes us as being singularly courageous:

Her owner and his assistants, after a short deliberation, followed her upon their hands and knees, with lighted candles, and having placed a sack on the ground near her, they made her lie down upon it; they then tied her four legs and passed a cord round her mouth, which they secured; in this state they drew her out from under the granary, upon the sack, and then she was lifted and carried by six men into her den in the caravan. To the astonishment of everyone who beheld this part of the transaction (which lasted about a quarter of an hour), the lioness lay as quietly as a lamb during her removal to the caravan; but when she was there she became sensible of the restraints she was under, and her rage was excessive till the cords which annoyed her were loosened.

I do not think I would care to crawl under a barn and try to persuade a lioness, who had just savaged a dog and a horse, to lie on a sack while I tied up her jaws, especially with only the light of a guttering candle to work by! An eye-witness account however, says that throughout this breathless operation she was as one dazed.

What of the coach passengers? As the unknown animal made her first leap they fled into the inn, barring the door behind them, but one of them was too slow. When the hubbub was over and they unbarred the door, there he was, in a state of panic and exhaustion. The lioness had actually brushed against him when she turned upon the dog. The man recovered sufficiently to give his account of the affair to the newspaper but after a few days collapsed completely. He spent the remaining 27 years of his life in the asylum at Laverstock.

Meantime the horse Pomegranate was purchased by the quick-witted menagerie owner and had a lamentable success at Salisbury Fair next day, exhibiting his wounds to the public.

Although a lively little story and one which might make headlines for a day, it is little more than an incident. It is difficult to understand why the story so caught the public fancy. But there is no doubt that it did. The lioness of

Winterslow Hutt became known all over the country, and quite a flood of paintings, especially painted trays, were turned out. The Pheasant Inn naturally made a collection of them and could show the visitor half a dozen or more until, quite recently, one proprietor, retiring, took them with him. On the stairs there used to stand a large oil-painting of the adventure, with the lioness clawing the horse, which, however, is standing not outside The Pheasant but outside an inn in London. Apparently the tale was such good publicity that other pubs unashamedly commandeered it for their own use.

Oddly enough, a parallel instance occurred at the other end of Wiltshire, at Malmesbury, a hundred years earlier. A maid from The White Lion Inn, visiting a travelling menagerie in the town and standing too near the tiger's den, was seized by the tiger and so badly mauled that she died. Her name was Hannah Twynnoy, and she was thirty-three years old when the mishap occurred, on 23 October 1703. She is remembered by a monument which still stands in Malmesbury churchyard, bearing the inscription:

> In bloom of life she's snatched from hence;
> She had not room to make defence;
> And here she lyes in bed of clay,
> Until the Resurrection Day.

4   More Stories of the Highway

Some of the stories attached to Dick Turpin really belong to a Wiltshire highwayman, Thomas Boulter. Black Bess was actually the name of Boulter's horse. He stole her from Erlestoke Park one night and she carried him for years. Mounted presumably on Black Bess, he rode eighty miles from Windsor to his home at Poulshot. Usually he changed horses at intervals on a long journey, as highwaymen normally did, but on this occasion he rode the same animal all the way, holding up three coaches between Windsor and Maidenhead while being closely pursued all the time.

Born in 1748, he was the son of the miller at Poulshot. He worked at his father's mill until he was twenty-six years old and then moved to the Isle of Wight, where he started a milliner's shop. Finding that he was losing more money than he was making, he became a highwayman.

He started on the Great West Road, holding up a coach between Stockbridge and Salisbury. We know a great deal about his career and what his feelings were because, in the condemned cell, he was granted a three weeks' reprieve to write his confessions, or memoirs. He seems to have been a sensitive, indeed timid, man who was always polite to his victims and apparently never hurt anyone. In Wiltshire he was popularly known as a 'gentleman of the road'.

On one occasion he escaped from prison by cutting a hole in the prison wall. Once, after having seized £500, he rode from Blandford to Exeter in a day, via Weymouth and

Honiton. Arrested and sentenced to death, he was reprieved on condition that he joined the army, but his military service lasted just four days before he absconded.

Although his financial difficulties soon disappeared, the excitement of his new way of life made it impossible for him to return to the dull business of shopkeeping. Maybe his upbringing had something to do with it, for his father had once been whipped in Devizes market-place for robbing an old woman, and his brother had been a highwayman too, until crippled in a hold-up. At last Thomas's luck ran out. He was betrayed at Bridport and was hanged at Winchester on 19 August 1778.

Boulter was one of a succession of notorious highwaymen. Three of the most celebrated were operating in the last two decades of the seventeenth century. One was James Whitney, whose father, the former rector of Donhead St Andrew, had been evicted under the Commonwealth for Royalist sympathies. Whitney was a more ruthless character than Boulter. He formed a gang strong enough to fight pitched battles with any victims who resisted, as happened when on one occasion they held up the Oxford stage-coach. Once the gang got away with £15,000, which, allowing for the difference in currency values, must have been more or less on a par with the Great Train Robbery. Eventually they were captured by a troop of dragoon guards and were hanged at Smithfield.

Biss was another highwayman from a well-to-do family. He was said to be the son of the vicar of Bishopstrow, whose family owned property at Upton Scudamore and Tisbury. He had the reputation of being a Robin Hood, robbing the rich but helping the poor, but his end was predictable. He was hanged at Salisbury in 1695.

William Davis, yet another highwayman, was hanged at Tyburn in 1689. He was not a Wiltshireman but conducted most of his operations on Salisbury Plain. Like other 'gentlemen highwaymen' he was reasonably prosperous and owned a farm and an inn. His career apparently lasted nearly forty years – unusually long for such a hazardous profession.

Wiltshire also had its own highwaywoman, whose career, as it happened, was very short. Mary Sandall was a Baverstock woman, aged about 24. She apparently went out on the road from a sense of adventure, since she could afford a horse, and her hauls were trifling. Armed with a pistol and dressed as a man, she held up a neighbour, a Mrs Thring of Burcombe, and robbed her of two shillings and a black silk cloak. The alarm was raised, and Mary was soon caught. She was tried and sentenced to death but was reprieved.

Until the middle of the nineteenth century grain was commonly sold in pitched markets, as distinct from selling by sample. Farmers took their entire harvest to market and bargained with buyers on the spot. Salisbury, Devizes and Warminster were outstanding examples of pitched markets, with Warminster predominant. As many as 2,000 quarters (4,000 sacks) of wheat were sold there weekly at the height of the season, and there are memories of teams of horses struggling to haul the great, heavily-laden waggons up the steep incline by the church, often axle-deep in mud.

Farmers used to like striking a bargain and receiving payment in cash the same day. 'Generally before three o'clock,' says one comment, thus allowing plenty of time to get home before dark – an important consideration before bank-notes and cheques came into general use and large sums had to be carried in the form of guineas.

One hazard likely to be encountered is illustrated by a memorial stone, often hidden by long grass, that stands at the junction of the Devizes highway with the by-road to the abandoned village of Imber. The interesting inscription records that:

At this spot Mr Dean of Imber was attacked and robbed by four highwaymen in the evening of October 21st, 1839.

After a spirited pursuit of three hours one of the felons, Benjamin Colclough, fell dead on Chitterne Down. Thomas Saunders, George Waters and Richard Harris were eventually captured, and were convicted at the ensuing Quarter Sessions at Devizes and transported for a term of fifteen years. This monument is erected by public subscription as a warning to those who presumptuously think to escape the punishment God has threatened against Thieves and Robbers.

Mr Dean, of Imber, was evidently a farmer on his way home from Devizes market with some harvest money in his pocket. There is a vivid elaboration extant of the story. On being held up by the four highwaymen Farmer Dean proposed a wager.

'I'll bet,' he said, 'that I'm a better shot than any of you lot. Look,' he continued, 'we'll throw my hat in the air, and the one who puts most holes in it before it touches the ground takes the money.'

They agreed, and the firing began.

'Wait a bit,' said one of the highwaymen as he retrieved the much-battered hat. 'The pistols are empty.'

'Mine aren't!' said Farmer Dean. 'Hands up!'

The story of the subsequent chase reveals one interesting fact. It appears that, contrary to the popular image of highwaymen as cavalier-type gentlemen on horseback, these robbers were on foot. No doubt Farmer Dean was mounted and was doubtless able to enlist reinforcements during the pursuit. The names and behaviour of the felons would seem to indicate that these were local men, and, in view of the date, soon after the machinery riots of 1830, were hard put to earn an honest penny.

5   The Tale of the Weaver

This is the narrative related by Thomas Goddard of
Marlborough, on 23 November 1674, and deposed by him
in the presence of Christopher Lypiatt, Mayor, Ralph
Baily, Town Clerk, and Joshua Sacheverell, Rector of St
Peter's:

He saith that on Monday, the ninth inst, as he was going to
Ogbourne, at a stile on the highway near Mr Goddard's
ground, by nine in the morning he met the apparition of
his father-in-law, one Edward Avon of this town, glover,
who died in May last, having on, to all appearances, the
same clothes, hat, stockings and shoes as he did usually
wear when he was living, standing by and leaning over
that stile. As Goddard came near, the apparition spoke to
him with an audible voice these words, 'Are you afraid?'

To which he answered, 'I am thinking of one who is
dead, observing whom you are like.'

To which the apparition replied, 'I am he that you were
thinking of. I am Edward Avon, your father-in-law. Come
near to me; I will do you no harm.'

Goddard answered, 'I trust in him who hath bought my
soul, you shall do me no harm.'

Then the apparition asked, 'How do William and Mary?'
meaning his son, William Avon, a shoemaker here, and
Mary, his daughter, the said Goddard's wife.

Then it said, 'What, Taylor is dead!' meaning one Taylor
of London, who had married his daughter Sarah and died
about Michaelmas last. Then the apparition held out its

hand, and in it, as Goddard conceived twenty or thirty shillings in silver, and spake in a loud voice,

'Take this money and send it to Sarah, for I shut up the bowels of compassion toward her in my lifetime and now here is somewhat for her.'

And then said, 'Mary is troubled for me, but tell her I have received mercy contrary to my deserts.'

But Goddard answered, 'I refuse all such money.'

Upon which the apparition said, 'I perceive you are afraid. I will meet you some other time', and immediately it went away up the lane. So Goddard went over the same stile, but saw it no more that day.

The next night about seven o'clock it came, and opened Goddard's shop-window and stood in the same clothes as before, looking him in the face but saying nothing. And the next night after, as Goddard went forth into his back premises with a candle-light in his hand, it appeared to him again in the same shape, but, being in fear, he ran into his house and saw it no more then.

But on Thursday, the 12th inst, as he came from Chilton, riding down the hill between the Manor House and Axford Farm field, he saw something like a hare crossing his way, at which his horse, being frightened, threw him in the dirt. As soon as he could recover his feet, the same apparition met him again and, standing about eight feet directly before him in the way, spake again to him in a loud voice.

'Source (a word he commonly used when living) you have stayed long: Thomas, bid William Avon take the sword that he had of me, which is now in his house, and carry it to the wood as we go to Alton, to the upper end of the wood by the wayside; for with that sword I did wrong about thirty years ago, and he has never prospered since he had that sword. And bid William Avon give his sister Sarah twenty shillings of the money he had of me. And do you talk with Edward Lawrence for I borrowed twenty shillings of him several years ago and did say I had paid him, but I did not. And I would desire you to pay him out of the money which you had from James Elliott at two payments (which money the said Goddard now saith was £5) which Elliott, a baker, owed to the deceased Avon on bond, and which he had received from Elliott since Michaelmas in two payments, 35 shillings at one payment and £3 and 5 shillings at another payment.'

And it further said to him,

'Tell Margaret (his widow) that I would desire her to deliver up the little which I gave to little Sarah Taylor, either to the child herself or to anyone she will trust for it. And see that this be done within a twelvemonth and a day after my decease, and peace be with you.'

And so it went away over the rails into the wood, and he saw it no more at that time. And he saith that he paid the twenty shillings to Edward Lawrence, of this town, who, being present now, doth remember that he lent the deceased twenty shillings about twenty years ago, which none knew but himself and his wife, and Avon and his wife, and that it had never been repaid to him until now.

And this said Goddard further saith that this very day, by Mr Mayor's orders, he with his brother-in-law William Avon went with the sword; and about nine o'clock this morning laid it down in the copse near the place the apparition had appointed. Then, coming away, Goddard, looking back, saw the apparition in like habit as before. Whereupon he called to his brother-in-law, 'Here is the apparition of our father.'

Who said, 'I see nothing.'

The apparition beckoned to Goddard and said, 'Thomas, take up the sword and follow me.'

And so he took up the sword and followed it about ten lugs further into the copse. Then Goddard, laying down the sword upon the ground, saw something stand by the apparition like a mastiff dog of a brown colour. Then the apparition coming towards him, Goddard stepped back about two steps.

The apparition said to him, 'I have permission to you and commission not to touch you.'

And it took up the sword and went to the place at which before it stood, with the mastiff dog by it as before, and pointing the top of the sword in the ground said,

'In this place lies buried the body of him which I murdered in the year 1635, which is now rotten and turned to dust.'

Whereupon Goddard said, 'I do adjure you, wherefore did you this murder?'

It said, 'I took money from the man, and he contended with me, and so I murdered him.'

Then Goddard said, 'What would you have me do in this thing?'

And the apparition said, 'This is that the world may know that I murdered a man and buried him in this place in the year 1635.'

Then the apparition laid down the sword and, rushing further into the copse, vanished; and he saw it no more.

6   Houses, Inns and Churches

One of the most celebrated or notorious ghosts is that of Will Darrell, 'Wild Darrell', who although he lived in Elizabethan times still haunts the place where he met his death. His story is recalled by every book on Wiltshire.

One stormy night a midwife, Mother Barnes of Shefford, in Berkshire, was awakened and offered a lavish reward to attend the confinement of a Lady Kenvytt. She accompanied the messenger, riding pillion. After they had travelled seven or eight miles over the Downs her companion stopped and insisted on blindfolding her, informing her that it was not Lady Kenvytt who had summoned her.

They arrived at a country mansion where the blindfold was removed and Mother Barnes was escorted to a bedroom where, in a four-poster bed, lay a masked lady in the last stages of labour. She duly assisted with the delivery and wrapped the baby, a boy, in her apron, watched by a tall, saturnine man dressed in black velvet.

She left the room for a few moments, looking for some clothes for the baby, but on her return the tall man stepped forward and ordered her to put the child on the log fire blazing on the hearth. Appalled, she refused, begging on her knees to be allowed to keep the baby, whereupon the man thrust her roughly aside and threw the child on the fire, stirring it with his boot. She was then allowed to attend to the mother and, when she had done all she could, was blindfolded again and so escorted to her cottage, receiving in payment a bag of gold.

With considerable presence of mind she had, while attending to her patient, snipped a piece off the bedcover and also counted the number of stairs. Next morning she went to a local magistrate with the story. Suspicion fell on Darrell, and the material from the bedcover was found to match exactly. The house was Littlecote House.

Darrell was arrested and tried for murder. To general surprise, he was acquitted. One version of the story has it that the judge at the trial was his kinsman who agreed to set him free in return for the Littlecote estate. Another, that the judge used his influence with the Attorney General of that time, with whom he was very friendly. Rumour suggested that the mother of the baby was Darrell's sister and that he was therefore guilty of incest.

Anyhow, acquitted he was, and a few months later was thrown from his horse and broke his neck, at a place still called Darrell's Stile. Everyone regarded this as deserved retribution. The judge at his trial, Judge Popham, inherited the property and bequeathed it to his descendants.

Naturally, the story has accumulated its quota of ghost stories. Most popular was the one that the horse shied at the ghost of the murdered child. The ghost of Darrell is still sometimes seen, and the site of his death is said to be haunted by ghostly hounds, in full cry after his soul. The ghosts of the mother and baby have both been seen at various times in the bedroom and on the landing, while the ghost of the midwife may be seen kneeling by the fireplace.

In about 1861 the heir to Littlecote, a small boy named Francis Popham, was lying ill in a room over the entrance to the house. The nurse, alarmed by his condition, sent an urgent message to his parents who were away visiting. The next night as she was keeping vigil by the child's bedside, she was greatly relieved to hear the gates flung open, the noise of a coach on the drive, and then the bell being rung vigorously. She waited for the parents to arrive and, when they failed to do so, she went to the casement window and threw it open. There was nothing to be seen – no coach, no horses, no one moving in the moonlight. Next day the parents arrived but their child was dead.

Years afterwards the child's father, searching through some documents in the muniments room, found an old manuscript which stated that, when the death of an heir to the estate was imminent, Wild Will Darrell would drive up to the door of the mansion with coach and horses!

In more recent times a spectral coach has been seen near a cottage in the woods about two miles from Littlecote.

A few years ago an elderly man was just breaking off work for his midday snack when he heard the sound of horses' hooves approaching. Expecting to see a coach and four, he stood back in a gateway to allow it to pass safely. Along came the coach, its interior brightly lit, and, suddenly, it disappeared! There was no corner or bend in the road.

In the evening he mentioned the occurrence at his local inn and was surprised to learn that several other persons claimed to have seen or heard a spectral coach at that very spot, not far from Littlecote Manor.

One of the latest manifestations of the supernatural was experienced by a Mr Wills who was acting as a guide to Littlecote. He was attracted by the sight of a woman in blue who was making her way up the stairs to the third floor, which was closed to the public by a rope. He made to accost her when to his consternation she passed straight through the rope! He was so disconcerted that he refused to continue to act as guide.

At Stanton St Bernard about a century or so ago the wife of a village farmer died and, in accordance with her wishes, was buried with several valuable rings on her fingers. This became widely known and the sexton was tempted to try to retrieve them. Accordingly after the funeral service, when all the mourners had returned home, he went down into the vaults and set to work on the coffin lid. Here, however, he encountered an obstacle – he was unable to detach the rings from the lady's finger. Losing his nerve, he attempted to cut off a finger – and the lady sat up!

Frightened out of his wits, the sexton stumbled out of the vault, leaving his lantern behind and the vault open. The lady managed to get out of the coffin by the light of the lantern and walked home, clad in her white shroud. She entered the house by the front door, crossed the hall and revealed herself to her astounded husband. Blood dripped from her finger on to the floor.

What happened to the rascally sexton is unrecorded, but the lady lived for some years after her resurrection and now haunts her former home on the anniversary of her first funeral. Several maids have at various times seen the ghost, emerging through the front door and standing by the dining-room door, her finger dripping blood. One dropped a trayful of china and another ran home screaming. There is a reluctance on the part of the residents to sit alone in the dining-room.

I have for a long time known the essentials of the murder story of Sutton Benger and of the apparitions that have subsequently appeared but am indebted to the Autumn 1991 edition of the magazine *Wiltshire Folklife*, the journal of the Wiltshire Folklife Society, for many of the details which follow. Although the events occurred 170 years ago they are fresh in the memory of old inhabitants of the village, who have no hesitation in pointing out the 'Murder Cottage', though in fact, the original cottage was demolished in about 1850.

The salient facts of the story are that a respectable widow was murdered by blows to the head with an axe. Goods taken from the cottage were found in the possession of a gipsy, Ted Buckland, the next morning. The story goes that the gipsy was immediately apprehended, taken to The Bell Inn, tried by a hastily assembled court and promptly executed outside. As a matter of fact, he was tried by a judge and jury and was publicly executed in Devizes market-place on 17 March 1821. The writer of the tale, Kay Taylor, has conducted painstaking research into what actually happened.

Ted Buckland was at the time sixty-seven years old 'with black hair, bushy grey whiskers and a long beard'. He was slightly built, very lean and only 5 feet 3 inches tall. He used to camp with a band of gipsies down a green lane in the parish but in the end he achieved such an evil reputation, 'was such a bad 'un that even his own tribe kicked him out'. Thereafter he lived a solitary life and was 'a common sight wandering the neighbourhood wrapped in a dirty old blanket tied round the waist with string and pinned across his chest with a meat skewer'. In summer he would go barefoot and sleep, wrapped in his blanket, in local gravel quarries. In winter he sometimes managed to persuade a local farmer to let him sleep in his barn, and sometimes in cold weather another farmer took pity on him and gave him some straw to lie on. He did odd jobs and went begging from house to house, mainly for salt, needles and tinder.

Mrs Judith Pearce, the murder victim, lived alone in an isolated cottage at the foot of Seagry Hill. She was fifty-eight years old and was employed at Church Farm, Seagry, doing domestic chores. She often shared her food with Ted Buckland, considering this her Christian duty, but always took advantage of her opportunity by lecturing him on his evil ways.

On one occasion Ted arrived at nightfall and demanded to be allowed in to sit by the fire, but his manner was so threatening that she slammed the door in his face. He stayed around for a time – she could hear him prowling about – but finding she had barred and bolted the doors securely he went away grumbling. That night the thatched roof of the cottage was set on fire. Fortunately a heavy storm of rain came on at the critical moment, and with the help of neighbours the fire was soon extinguished.

Buckland was arrested but for some reason was freed. He then disappeared for about six months but when he returned to the district it was widely believed he was seeking revenge on Judith Pearce. Judith felt so nervous she had her 12-year-old granddaughter, Elizabeth Cottle, to sleep with her.

Buckland was seen again in the neighbourhood in mid-November when he called on a charitable soul, a Mrs Ann Flowers, who gave him some of her husband's old clothes, including a greatcoat and breeches. That night Elizabeth and her grandmother, who slept in a room above the buttery, retired to bed at about seven o'clock. Some time later they were awakened by a noise, and Mrs Pearce went down to the buttery to investigate. She found nothing but could hear sounds of an intruder in the kitchen, so they both got dressed and barred the door.

In due course there came the noise of an axe battering at the door of the buttery and a hand appeared in the hole. The two women rushed to the gap and a sharp instrument was thrust through it, cutting Mrs Pearce over the eye and causing a rush of blood. Then for a short space of time silence reigned. Judith fetched her own hatchet with the idea of knocking a hole through the thin wall of the buttery and making their escape to the village for help.

They put the first part of the plan into operation but then ran into a snag. When Elizabeth clambered through the hole she had to release her hold on the furniture holding the door shut, and the door fell in. Judith and Elizabeth had to make a dash for it and were fleeing across the garden when their assailant struck. He first knocked Mrs Pearce to the ground and then grabbed Elizabeth, telling her to be quiet. However, she screamed and struggled free. He then turned his attention to the grandmother again and gave her three more blows to the head, while Elizabeth ran panting across the garden and into the fields.

She had to run about half a mile to her great-uncle's

house and noted that while she was blurting out her story the clock struck three. A party was quickly assembled, including her uncles William and Thomas, and made their way to the cottage, where they found Judith lying dead in the garden. It had taken about half an hour to fetch help. Elizabeth had no doubt as to the identity of the murderer as she knew Ted Buckland quite well, having often seen him begging in the neighbourhood.

At the trial she repeated her identification, to be greeted by an outburst from Buckland who accused her of being a 'damned liar'. 'I'll be damned if my life is to be sworn away by such a dirty, stinking little hussy as thee,' he said. But, though conducting his own defence, he refused to cross-examine her.

The Revd Charles Lipscombe, vicar of Sutton Benger, exhibited a model of the cottage that he had had made by the village carpenter and used it to explain the crime. Another witness produced the doorpost from the buttery door, showing the catch which had been burst open. Dr Joseph Hayward stated that death was caused by four wounds to the head and confirmed that they could have been caused by the corner of a hatchet.

At this stage some controversy developed over the hatchet. The landlord of The Bell Inn produced a hatchet on which were marks exactly matching cuts in the doorpost of the buttery. Buckland countered this by maintaining that he hadn't possessed a hatchet for three months. The one produced in court had been retrieved from the bottom of the brook.

This statement was flatly contradicted by a Mr William Greenwood, of Christian Malford, who said that only a week before Ted had offered him a hatchet in exchange for a hatful of potatoes. The hatchet had some lettering on it, which he was unable to read, being illiterate, and also a notch on the handle, exactly as the hatchet exhibited in court. He had not gone ahead with the transaction, being of the opinion that Buckland had not come by the hatchet honestly, but could swear that it was the same one. Buckland indignantly protested that Greenwood was 'a lying rascally whelp'. In conclusion Police Constable Ellery testified that dirt found on the greatcoat that Buckland had worn matched that from the wattle and daub walls of the cottage.

In his summing up of the case the judge admitted that, without the evidence of the hatchet, most of the evidence was circumstantial, but it took the jury only a minute to find Buckland guilty.

Ted Buckland was publicly hanged in Devizes market-place on 17 March 1821, protesting his innocence to the last. 'Upon my soul, I did not kill the old woman,' he said from the scaffold. Looking around he asked, 'Are any of my people here?' and then made his final request, 'Can't you hang me up a little and then let me down again!'

The murder attracted a good measure of publicity. A memorial stone was erected by public subscription over Judith's grave in Sutton churchyard, and may still be seen there, though the inscription is much weathered. And on 2 December 1820, the following poem was published in the *Bath Herald*:

A lonely cottage stands beside the way,
A white-thatched cot, with honeysuckles gay;
There JUDITH PEARCE, a widow lived alone,
By a rough quarry of blue-coloured stone;
Where lurked a wretch, of Egypt's wandering race,
A wretch forlorn, without a mark of grace
Whom ruffians left, for such a rogue was he
That even the vilest shunned his company;
Dark was his face, but darker still his mind
To pity, and to every tender feeling blind.
He had no friends, nor knew the joys of home,
But muttering, through the dews of night would roam,
Brooding on fancied wrongs, with secret pride,
On words, or looks, or benefits denied.
Round his gaunt side a rope for girdle swung,

From which a light, short-handled hatchet hung;
A tattered garment did the village fright,
A coat by day, a blanket by the night,
Which round his neck a butcher's skewer confined,
Fit fastening such a filthy dress to bind.
Judith had often a kind warning given,
How far his ways were from the ways of heaven;
And once, too, Judith (which would kindle strife
In greater persons) asked him – 'Where's your wife?'
Once fire denied – a common courtesy;
Yet there seemed danger in his quick black eye;
And so there was, for as she lay in bed
At night the thatch was blazing o'er her head,
And EDWARD BUCKLAND, so the villain call,
Was met in haste, close to the village wall;
As if on some villainy he mused
The evening salutation he refused;
Suspected, taken, he escapes at last,
And all supposed the danger now was past—
When Judith's brother, in the dead of night,
Heard his grand-niece, who shook with cold and fright
Tell how she 'scaped the murderer's hand by flight;
'Wake! Wake! she's murdered!' was the frightful cry;
'I heard the blow! I almost saw her die.'
They found her lying on the garden mould,
Mangled with dreadful wounds, quite dead and cold,
A sight to shock the weak, and almost scare the bold.

In view of the notoriety of the crime, spectral apparitions have been surprisingly few, and they all concern Ted Buckland rather than Judith Pearce.

One occurred around the turn of the century, eighty years after the events recounted. A girl of fifteen walking with two friends from Seagry to Sutton one winter night was alarmed by the apparition of a short man in a dirty, shapeless coat who walked across the road in front of her. She screamed but was laughed at by her companions who had seen nothing.

In exactly the same spot in the 1970s an instructor was

teaching an 18-year-old boy to drive when the lad suddenly swerved across the road, making it necessary for the man to grab the steering-wheel. 'But didn't you see that old man in a dirty old blanket walk across the road in front of us? I thought we were going to run him down.' The pupil was a newcomer to the district and had never heard of Judith Pearce or Edward Buckland. Yet the instructor, who was a native and knew the story well, saw nothing.

Recently a woman, driving home along the Seagry road to Great Somerford, thought she had hit a small man in a dirty old cloak. So convinced was she that she called a search party of friends and relatives who, however, found no trace of the man nor of any accident.

The following ghost stories are all historical in nature. They are concerned with events that occurred in houses, inns and churches a long time ago, though in many instances their repercussions are still felt.

The King and Queen Inn at Highworth is about 600 years old and was once a coaching inn. One night the landlord was clearing up after his customers had gone home when his two Alsatian dogs in the cobblestone yard started howling, quite unlike their normal barking.

When he went out to investigate, instead of rushing to greet him the dogs were crouching down, rigid, their tails sticking out and their hair bristling. The landlord looked in the direction in which they were staring and was in time to see the figure of a man, dressed as a monk, moving swiftly across the yard and disappearing through a wall! As soon as it had vanished the dogs were all right again, though it was noticeable that they didn't go to sniff at the wall.

The figure has been seen by other observers on various occasions.

In about the year 1624 a drunken man called at the

vicarage late one night and demanded the keys of the church, to ring a peal of bells. The vicar naturally refused. Apart from any other consideration, he said, it would arouse Sir George Wroughton, whose house adjoined the churchyard. The drunk stumbled off, grumbling and threatening to be revenged.

Some time later he met a man named Cantle or Cantlow, in Devizes, who had a reputation as a wizard. Having listened to the tale Cantle declared, 'Does he not love ringing? He shall have enough of it!' That night a bell began to toll in the vicarage.

Cantle was arrested and confined to Fisherton jail in Salisbury, where he remained for the rest of his life. He confessed that he caused the sound and declared that it would continue as long as he lived. The circumstances attracted a lot of attention, so much so that King James I sent a gentleman to the Wilcot rectory to report on the truth of the tale. The gentleman confirmed the ringing of the bell but said that when he put his head out of the window no sound could be heard. It was confined to the rectory.

There is a house in Steeple Ashton, reputed to be 600 years old, which was a court house in the reign of James II and is said to have been used by Judge Jeffreys, the judge who tried the rebels after the Battle of Sedgmoor in 1685.

Its ghost is a cloaked figure which lifts an iron latch on a bedroom door, enters the room and glides across it to an old corner cupboard. There it seems to be searching for something in the pigeon-holes. Several people have seen it, but who it is or what it is looking for no one knows.

Before its dissolution in the reign of Henry VIII Wilcot Manor was a monastery. It is said that when the brothers were dispossessed one, a very old monk, refused to leave. He had lived there all his life and knew no other home, so when the time came he withdrew to an upper chamber and hanged himself.

Since then he has appeared to several people visiting

the manor, a cowled figure who bends over a bed. A curious feature of the visitation, however, is that it appears only to those spending their first night in the manor. One was a butler engaged by Lady St Maur who was so alarmed that he refused to sleep there again and took a bedroom in a cottage nearby.

Echoes of a long-ago tragedy occur in All Cannings rectory, which was built by a Royalist rector in 1646. At the time of the Commonwealth the wife of the rector, Mrs Bynge, with her three small sons all under six years old, were turned out of the house by Cromwell's men.

Now the rectory is haunted by a 'grey lady' with 'a very sweet face'. She traverses an upstairs corridor and visits two bedrooms, one on either side of the house. She also descends, by way of a now demolished spiral staircase, to the kitchen and floats along a back passage to the gardens. In the past a number of maids have professed to have heard the swish of her silk skirts, and there have been recent reports of a 'grey lady' having been seen standing at the foot of a bed.

Manningford Bruce rectory is the scene of the enactment of a part of history.

In the chancel of the church is the tomb of Sir Edward Nicholas and his wife Mary, who was the sister of Jane Lane who assisted the escape of Charles II after the Battle of Worcester. She rode pillion behind him when he was disguised as her manservant. Afterwards Charles granted the Lane family the honour of bearing the lion from the Royal Arms on their armorial bearings, as can be seen on Mary Lane's tomb.

The ghost story concerns a Miss Coles, niece of the Reverend R.E. Coles, one-time rector of Manningford, who some time in the 1930s was sleeping in the room said to have once been occupied by King Charles. Waking in the small hours, her attention was attracted by a party of gentlemen, dressed in seventeenth-century fashion, seated around the fire playing cards. One of them closely resembled Charles II. Only half-awake, she dropped off again, to awake some time later to see the card game still in progress. She remembered the event in the morning, but there have been no subsequent occurrences.

An au pair girl recently had a shock when she saw the figure of a monk sitting in the library of Avebury House. To everybody's consternation she went to ask whether he was remaining for lunch. There was, of course, no one there. Avebury House, an Elizabethan manor, stands on the site of a Benedictine priory, founded in the eleventh century.

Another ghost story connected with Avebury is of a girl who, from an upstairs window, saw the figure of a man, wearing the costume of a Cavalier, walking in the garden.

A well-authenticated and well-known ghost concerns an Elizabethan marriage and subsequent dispute. Sir Walter Long, MP, had two families, one a son named John and a second named Walter, by his second wife. Lady Catherine, the second wife, conspired with her brother, Sir Egremont Thynne, of Longleat, to disinherit John in favour of the second son Walter.

As a lawyer was drawing up the deed incorporating the transaction he was terrified to see a lady's white hand interposed between his eyes and the parchment, preventing him from completing the document. Scared out of his wits, he refused to complete the deed, and another clerk had to be called in.

The story became widely known and resulted in the will being contested. In the end the matter was settled amicably, Walter retaining the Draycott property and John the estate at Wraxall.

And now the tale of an exorcism.

It concerns Wyke House, Trowbridge, which was built early in the seventeenth century. At some time just over a century ago one of the servants was saying goodnight to her sweetheart when a ghost appeared. They fled, terrified, and told the rest of the household, who gossiped about it so much that it was decided to exorcize the apparition.

They did the thing in style. Twelve Protestant clergymen were assembled at midnight and resorted to incantations to 'raise' the ghost. Apparently they were successful, for it appeared and was then given the choice of where it should be laid. It decided on a large chest, into which it climbed. The chest was then fastened down – and there the story ends. It would be interesting to know what happened to the chest.

Although it has nothing to do with this episode there is in a box in a lumber-room in an old mansion at Garsdon, near Malmesbury, a ghost that has been officially 'laid'.

The date of the following story is not known but, on reflection, it raises some sinister implications.

A lady, now deceased, lived as a girl with her parents and sisters in a cottage near the church of Bradford-on-Avon. One night one of the sisters heard noises like the jingling of coins in her bedroom, and, waking up, saw the figure of a man. It disappeared, and she went back to sleep. However, she saw the apparition again on several occasions before the family moved house. As it did not appear to be concerned with her she assumed that she must have been dreaming and fell asleep again. But she did tell her sisters about it.

A later tenant also saw the ghost and did not take the experience so calmly. He moved his bed downstairs and refused to sleep in the bedroom. Moreover he talked about it, arousing a good deal of speculation. People talked about robbery, hidden treasure and even murder, but no search was ever conducted.

Some time later the cottage, which dated from the seventeenth century, was being modernized when part of a skeleton was unearthed under a flagstone floor. The bones were obviously very old, and it was suggested that the ground on which the cottage was built had once been part of a churchyard. But the skeleton was buried only a few inches under the soil and not in a proper grave, and, moreover, the head pointed south-west, an unusual position for a Christian burial.

The police decided that in view of the age of the bones there was no need for an inquest, so the skeleton was reinterred. But speculation remains. Was a crime committed, followed by a hasty burial? And is that the cause for the haunting by the ghost?

Now a story which allows no rational explanation.

In 1946 Simon Harcourt-Smith and his family occupied Corsham priory, installing their two children there, with their nanny, while they themselves were abroad on business. The oldest child was aged three. When the parents returned this child recited to them a new prayer, which they recognized as the Ave Maria. The nanny was not Catholic, nor had the children been in contact with anyone else of the Catholic faith. Questioned about it, the child said he had been taught it by an old man dressed in white. Enquiries elicited that at about 1730 the priory was occupied by an order of white friars.

And now a tale from the Middle Ages. It concerns Pinkney Park, which is about a mile from Sherston and whose name is derived from Ralph de Pinkney, who once owned it.

The story, however, antedates Pinkney's reign and has its origins early in the fifteenth century. The park was then the subject of a dispute between two noble families, the Estcourts and the Cresswells, which involved litigation. What it was about and what the outcome was is forgotten. One version says that two sisters were involved and that one killed the other. From time to time a ghost is said to have been seen, carrying its head under its arm. On a door in the house is the print of a woman's hand and on the floor bloodstains, neither of which can be removed.

The most tangible evidence of the quarrel, and nobody now knows to which of the two families it belongs, is a skull. It is kept in a niche under a window by a flight of stairs. According to legend it is indestructible. It has been hammered to pieces and burnt and always returns, whole, to its accustomed perch. It is a small skull and said to be female.

There is a legend that asserts that when the Pinkney family becomes extinct and the property passes to strangers the skull will crumble into dust, but this must be a subsequent accretion, for the Pinkneys had not put in an appearance at the time of the original dispute.

There was once a party at the fourteenth-century manor-house, once the rectory, at Sutton Veny and as the house was very full the hostess asked one of the guests if she would mind sharing her room with her little sister. The girl had no objection and in due course retired for the night, the little sister being tucked into a cot by the bed. In the night the girl awoke with the feeling of a child's head resting on her shoulder. She thought that her sister must have crept into her bed but on striking a light saw that she was sound asleep in her cot. She went back to sleep but was awakened with the same impression – that a child's head was resting on her shoulder. But again her little sister was sleeping peacefully.

She couldn't get to sleep again and in the morning related her experience to her hostess. The next night the same thing happened, so for the rest of her stay another room was found for her.

Some years later the girl was telling her story in another place when another guest overheard and intervened. She said that at one time she and her husband had bought the old manor at Sutton Veny but had so much trouble with that part of the house that they had the wing pulled down. When the workmen were demolishing it they found under the floor a cavity in which were the skeletons of five children!

The Old Bell Inn at Malmesbury has a familiar apparition – a 'grey lady' who has been seen many times. A recent occasion was when a figure 'in flowing robes' appeared on a landing and vanished through a wall. She has also been seen on the main staircase and outside the inn, where she passes through a hedge growing alongside. A resident who was born at the inn and lived there for many years said no matter how many times the hedge was replanted the place through which the grey lady passed always died.

When alterations were made to The Old Bell in 1889 an underground passage was found and in it human bones. There were also several stone coffins. There is naturally speculation about whether the skeleton is that of the grey lady but nobody knows.

And now for some more 'grey ladies'.

A grey lady, supposed to be a former abbess, haunts Beckington abbey, and a nun walks in the priory gardens of the Priory of St Mary, at Kington St Michael, at 1.30 each morning.

A nun dressed in white may be seen in the church at Stratton St Margaret, and another in the church at Highworth.

In 1872 the skeleton of a woman was found bricked up in a cavity of the chancel wall at Purton church. It is believed to be that of a nun who continues to haunt the church from time to time.

The following story is contemporary but appears to have its origins in the distant past.

From 1937 onwards the RAF requisitioned a house at Upavon in which it installed Air Commodore D'Arcy Greig, who lived there for some years. On three occasions footsteps were heard coming across a paved yard, entering the house and going upstairs. Two Alsatian dogs were visibly scared. And on each occasion within a few days the air commodore was notified of the death of a close friend.

Sometimes he woke up in the night to hear the sound of distant church bells, and once, looking out of a window, he saw illuminated stained glass windows, where no house now exists. As he watched the windows vanished, though the church bells could still be heard.

Later, he learned that the place where the windows had appeared was the former site of a Benedictine priory.

We now come to a large group of stories that are more or less contemporary. In many instances the ghost cannot be identified with an historical personage. And many are just isolated incidents of something uncanny. All have occurred in old houses, inns or churches.

A lady living at Calne was, in her youth, a ringer at Calne church, which has eight bells. When a ringer happened to be absent, leaving only seven ringers, they would hear footsteps mounting the tower steps. They would pause at their work, waiting for a colleague to join them, but there was no one there. This happened on several occasions, giving rise to speculations that some long-dead ringer was attempting to help them.

The following story might be called The Mystery of the Unbroken Glasses.

On Christmas Day 1972, Mrs Blanche Chirgwin, wife of the manager of the Clifton Hotel, Swindon, was serving drinks at lunch-time behind the lounge bar. Behind her were several shelves of glasses, pushed well back because of traffic vibration. Suddenly, a tall, short-stemmed sherry glass rose clear of the shelf and, in a graceful curve, descended to the floor, where it spun round several times before coming to rest, quite unharmed. The floor is covered with hard red lino calculated to shatter into small fragments any glass falling on it.

The next day, Boxing Day, watched by a good number of customers, a second sherry glass descended in exactly the same manner, at exactly the same time. Mrs Chirgwin herself happened to see it. So did a young mongrel, Bonny, who was scared to death, rushing to the lounge bar door and scratching frantically to get out.

Since then tales have multiplied. A previous landlord

has remembered that once he found a window, which had been jammed for years, wide open. People going down to the cellars have reported a feeling that someone was following them. A shadowy hooded form is said to have been seen at a window. The inn is said to stand on the site of an old priory.

After the death of her father, Archdeacon Cockin, Mrs G.E.Montagu of Wilcot, distinctly saw him in his robes, standing behind the clergyman who was performing the Communion service in the chancel of Wilcot church.

At Easterton, near the Urchfont boundary, is the site of a vanished eighteenth-century house which was the home of the Wroughton family. The last member of the family was a recluse around whom various unsavoury stories have gathered, as, for instance, the question of what happened to several servant girls who mysteriously disappeared when in his service.

Finally he met his doom when, returning home drunk in a carriage drawn by four black horses, he overturned the carriage in his driveway and was killed. His house was never occupied again and eventually fell into ruin. But now, on a certain night said to be the anniversary of his death, the sound of galloping horses and the rattle of chains may be heard in the driveway leading to the ruins.

In September 1972, a Miss Marjorie Ashbery who lived at a house called Campfield, on the outskirts of All Cannings, was alone in the house when, from her bed, she saw the figure of a young fair-haired woman in a green dress. The apparition descended two non-existent steps and then faded away.

Miss Ashbery made enquiries and learned that many years earlier the house was occupied by a carrier married to a much younger woman. She was somewhat flighty and used to entertain other men while her husband was on his errands to Devizes. She did it once too often and was caught by her husband, who killed her, afterwards attempting to burn the house down.

Since then the ghost of the wife has at times returned to haunt the place.

Years ago a cottage in the village of Newton Tony was reputed to be haunted. People heard something which sounded like the old bread oven falling out and rolling about the floor. And there were sounds of crockery tumbling off the dresser.

Eventually a bricklayer was called in to repair the oven, and while he was examining it he found a round wooden bowl inside, of the sort that used to be often used as a till. He was disappointed, he said, at finding it empty but took it home as a curio. However, from that time the bricklayer never seemed short of money. And his deaf and dumb daughter told a friend, by signs, that the bowl had been full of coins. Still, the ghost was laid. The oven and the china ceased rolling about.

On 5 May 1852, little Francis Saville Kent was murdered by his half-sister Constance. An old man who had once worked in the house where the murder occurred said he had often heard 'a child crying and moaning' as he was about his work. The child is buried in East Coulston churchyard.

At Corsham in a house now demolished the figure of an old man used to appear, passing through a solid wall. In about 1895, a small girl would sit at the bottom of the stair and wait for the old man to appear, but her grandparents could see neither the ghost nor the door. When the house was demolished the skeleton of an elderly man was discovered bricked up in the wall at the point where the ghost had appeared.

In a similar incident in a cottage at Upavon a female ghost was seen every year on Lady Day, 25 March, but was visible only to a woman. Naturally no one would stay in the house on that date. When, in recent years, the house was pulled down the skeleton of a woman was discovered bricked up in the walls.

An old house at Braydon had recently been renovated,

before which it used to be the village forge. One night, at about one o'clock, a group of young people were standing outside the door, talking, when they noticed a man dressed in working clothes standing nearby. He wore a cloth cap and carried a sack over his shoulder. One drew attention to him and asked who he was, but the conversation moved to some other topic, and when they looked again the man had disappeared. They were surprised that he had vanished so quickly.

Next day one of the party described the man to her husband, who immediately exclaimed, 'Why, that was old John Aldridge, who used to live there!' He was the village blacksmith, and he used to carry his tools in a sack, slung over his shoulder by his hammer.

A Cherhill lady had a husband ill in bed. While her sister was sitting in her home she saw the figure of a man approaching. He lifted his foot as though to enter the room but drew back and disappeared. When this lady herself became very ill the sister saw the same figure. Again he came to the threshold and lifted his foot to cross it but evidently thought better of it, as he drew back and vanished.

This seems like a premonition of death but it didn't work out as might have been anticipated. The lady who was so ill recovered; it was the husband who died!

A house in Chippenham is haunted by a young woman who had many men friends, chiefly farmers attending the market. Eventually the inevitable happened; she found herself pregnant. Abandoned, she threw herself to her death from a window in her room. Since then the room is said to be unlucky. Any young woman who is pregnant is said to have an uncontrollable urge to throw herself out of the window into the street below.

A man working at Avebury manor was returning home by a footpath past Truslow manor when, by an iron gateway, he was accosted by a lady dressed in white, with a white hood. She had a lovely face but suddenly took him by the shoulder, turned him round and pushed him away from the gate. A lady who lives at Avebury had a similar experience. No explanation is forthcoming.

An evil ghost is said to haunt the new house occupying the site of Flower Farm, demolished in 1967. She (it is an unpleasant old woman) has been transferred from Flower Farm, haunting the upstairs room corresponding to the haunted one in the old farmhouse. She is actively evil, since five men working on the site of houses under construction in the area have experienced nasty accidents.

There was a story attached to the haunting, but it has been forgotten, the only person knowing the facts having died without divulging them. The presence, however, is described as being felt rather than seen. Workmen engaged on the site and knowing nothing of the story have said they felt there was 'a jinx on the place'.

The following is the story of an uneventful haunting of a hundred years ago which is, nevertheless, inexplicable except in terms of the supernatural.

A young clergyman who had been out visiting parishioners arrived home late at his lodgings and crept quietly upstairs so as not to disturb the other people. On the landing he met an elderly lady dressed in old-fashioned clothes and greeted her with a 'Good evening, madam'. Whereupon the lady immediately vanished.

Next morning at breakfast he happened to comment on the attractions of the old house and found his landlady quite enthusiastic about it. In private conversation with her husband later, however, he learned that he was not so sure. He too had seen the ghost on the landing, but his wife never had and laughed at him for having a vivid imagination.

This happened at Southwick, near Trowbridge, which is quite near the Box Tunnel. A short time afterwards there was an accident in the tunnel and the clergyman and a colleague who was sharing his lodgings debated whether they should go to bed, anticipating that they might be called to the scene. Eventually they went upstairs and one of them was surprised to see a young woman lying on the bed, her leg sticking out at an odd angle. His colleague, however, could not see her. They started to discuss the phenomenon when a policeman arrived and asked them to come to the scene of the disaster, as several persons were asking for a priest. When they arrived they were astounded to find, among the injured, the same young girl whom one of them had seen on the bed. Her leg was sticking out at the same dreadful angle and she was so badly injured that she was not expected to survive. She knew of her plight and had asked to see a clergyman.

White Rose Cottage, at All Cannings, was a pretty thatched and half-timbered cottage where, many years ago, lived an old couple, William and Ruth King. They were reputed locally to be quite well off, but when the old lady, who outlived her husband, eventually died, no money could be found. Then began the hauntings, which the villagers said was the old lady looking for, or guarding, her hidden hoard.

There was a succession of tenants in the cottage, none of whom was familiar with the story until events occurred which required explanation. One said she saw an old lady in a black dress going from bedroom to bedroom. Another said someone entered her room while she was in bed and smoothed down the eiderdown. Another refused to use the downstairs sitting-room as she felt unwelcome there.

One said she had felt nothing mysterious or uncanny except that a square of plaster on the ceiling kept falling down. In the end she called in the village handyman to repair it, and he discovered behind it a cavity. In it was a cardboard box, which was opened to great excitement. But all it contained was a pair of old-fashioned lady's stays and an old empty purse. And the plaster still persists in falling!

A lady living at The Manor, West Lavington, woke one

night to see a circle of light illuminating her room. In it she could discern the face of a very beautiful woman, haloed by a mass of auburn hair and wearing a blue gown. The visitor smiled at her, and she, thinking she had forgotten to switch off the light, turned to make sure. Her attention was distracted only momentarily, but in that brief moment the figure had disappeared.

Many years ago a cottage in Burbage was inhabited by a Mr and Mrs Grant, an elderly couple. It was a very old house and had in one of the bedrooms an upright post in the middle of the floor, reaching up to the ceiling. The Grant's bed was pushed up against this beam. At times the windows of this room would glow, as though illuminated by a light within the room. Mrs Grant said that at such times she saw an old woman, wearing a white apron over a dark, long-skirted gown and carrying a lighted candle in a candlestick, walk around the central beam. Mr Grant, however, saw nothing and ridiculed the idea.

'How can she walk around the beam when the bed is up against it?' he challenged.

'She walks right through it,' retorted Mrs Grant.

Mr Grant made enquiries of previous tenants and learned that they too had seen strange lights. Nobody had seen anything else except the eldest boy. He said he had seen an old woman clad in a dark, long-skirted dress and a white apron, carrying a lighted candle in a candlestick, in the bedroom.

'But then he's such a little liar,' said his family.

Now they were not so sure.

In the gardens of the old monastery at Edington a new house has been built, and a figure, thought to be that of an old monk, has been seen on a path leading from the church to the monks' well. The interesting thing is that the owner's dog, who barks at everything else, pays no attention to it.

Forty years ago, in a house very near to the old

monastery at Marlborough, a housewife was working rather late one night. She was putting the final touches to her tasks and had just put down a dish of water for the cat, Tinker Bell, when a hand clapped down on her shoulder.

'Is that you?' she asked, thinking it was her husband – and then, glancing round, saw there was no one there. The cat fled upstairs, terrified, and the lady quickly followed her. The husband, though, laughed at her and said she was quite mad.

The following story is of premonitions – or something more.

A Mrs F. Hues was in her bedroom at Cliff Farm, All Cannings, one afternoon in 1946 when, happening to glance out of the window, she saw an old man, Joshua Cowdry, who lived in a house opposite, enter his garden gate. He walked up the path leading to his back door and went inside.

Later at tea-time, Mrs Hues remarked to her husband that 'old Josie' must be better now. He had been ill in Devizes hospital but had been allowed to come home, as she had seen him that very afternoon. Mr Hues stared at her in amazement.

'He died this afternoon,' he told her.

Comparing times, they realized his death must have occurred at the time she saw him come home.

During an archaeological dig at Porch House, Potterne, a lady who was assisting with the finds came out of her bedroom one evening and went downstairs, passing the bedroom of her hostess. She happened to glance into the room as she passed and saw a figure sitting in a chair by the bedside. She naturally assumed it was her hostess and was very surprised to find her downstairs. They both went upstairs immediately, only to find the bedroom quite empty.

Two children who were staying at a house in Lacock begged to be allowed to change rooms, saying they were 'frightened at the ugly little man who came into their room at night'. Their request was granted. Some time later a wall between two bedrooms was being demolished during renovations and a second wall was found to have been constructed behind it. Under this wall was a human skeleton.

The owners of the house were away at the time so the builders simply rebuilt the wall without making any enquiries.

At Corsham Court in west Wiltshire a maid was scrubbing the back stairs when, looking up, she saw a lady on the landing, obviously waiting to descend. The maid quickly picked up her bucket and went to the foot of the stairs, standing aside to let her pass. No one came, so she looked up to see why. There was no one there!

Early in the nineteenth century a tragedy occurred at the rectory at Lydiard Millicent. A girl saw her lover, curate of the parish, murdered there. Later she married Sir Ferdinando Blunt, with whom she lived happily, but the memory of the tragedy was evidently very strong, for every year, on 30 October, the date of the murder, she is said to visit the garden and sit there under her favourite tree.

The following story is unusual in that it concerns actual physical contact with a ghost.

Some years ago a lady, then a little girl, was staying with her sister at her grandfather's house, a lodge belonging to Tottenham House, the seat of the Marquis of Ailesbury in Savernake Forest. One night she woke up with a start, thinking she heard her little sister calling. She jumped out of bed and ran along a passage to her sister's bedroom, but on the way she met an elderly lady dressed in very old-fashioned clothes. She was running so fast that she was unable to stop and so collided with the lady. Or rather, she would have collided if there had been anything to collide with. There was nothing. She ran straight through the figure!

A lady staying at Steeple Ashton vicarage, in the old

part of the house, woke in the middle of the night to find herself extraordinarily cold, though the weather was pleasantly warm. As she lay there, half-asleep, she heard a series of bangs overhead, as though someone were falling downstairs. She took the precaution of locking her door and presently fell asleep again.

The next morning, when she told her hosts, the vicar and his wife, they confessed to her that a former vicar's library was housed in an attic above the room where she had slept. When this room had a new occupant the books were hurled about in some confusion, as though someone disapproved. The vicar, his wife and their visitor went upstairs to the attic and, unlocking the door, found the books scattered all over the room in the wildest confusion, although on the previous evening they had been tidily arranged on their shelves.

A lady staying with her husband at Hinton manor was passing along a corridor outside the music-room when she heard the sound of music and peeped in. There she saw a lady in a long ruby-red dress playing on the spinet. The lady looked up and smiled at her.

The guest went back to her own room and complained to her husband that she had not been informed that they were wearing full evening-dress that evening.

'Oh, but we aren't,' he said.

'Well, why was the lady playing the spinet in the music-room wearing a long gown?' she demanded.

'Oh, so you've seen the Red Lady,' he told her.

Apparently the Red Lady was a recognized phenomenon, seen at irregular intervals, but who she was no one knows.

7 Ghosts on the Downs

Here we are back into history – or rather prehistory. That is understandable, for there are few human habitations on the Downs, although there used to be.

An old shepherd who kept his flock on Cherhill Down told Kathleen Wiltshire that he had seen a lot of men marching along an old Roman way.

'And they did wear skirts,' he added.

'*Were* they men?' she asked.

'Oh yes, they did have beards, some of 'em,' said the old man. 'And they wore gurt helmets, with 'air across the top. And they had a gurt bird on a pole a-front of em.'

The obvious conclusion is that these were Roman legionaries, marching behind their regimental eagle.

At Woodmanton legend has it that there was a great battle between the invading Romans and the British, presumably the Durotriges. The valley between two hills at a place called Patty's Bottom is said to have flowed with blood. Now on moonlit nights one can hear the sound of much tramping, and even headless horses can be seen careering about.

Here is a story which can be verified, though it happened over a hundred years ago. It was told to Kathleen Wiltshire by a lady in 1940 about her grandfather who, as a shepherd boy, watched his sheep near the Wansdyke near All Cannings.

On this dark night he and the shepherds with him

suddenly heard sounds of men and horses approaching along the Wansdyke and they wondered who it could be at that time of night. Then the moon came out from behind a cloud and revealed a party of men, carrying torches and walking behind a waggon drawn by black horses. On the waggon lay a coffin, strapped in position, and on the coffin a circlet or crown of gold.

Scared out of his wits, the lad fled and 'never stopped running till he reached the village'. The men, however, stood their ground and were amazed to see it vanish as it drew level with them.

When Miss Wiltshire was telling this story to Marlborough Townswomen's Guild a member told how her father, when courting her mother, had to pass near the Wansdyke where it leads near the village of Huish, and one night he saw the same funeral procession as described by the All Cannings' shepherds. This would have happened over a hundred years ago.

Miss Wiltshire speculates about the royal funeral and wonders whether it could have been that of Queen Guinevere who died at Amesbury nunnery and whose corpse was conveyed to Glastonbury, there to rest by the side of her husband, Arthur. The funeral procession was led by Sir Launcelot, who had with him eight men and a horse-bier, with 'torches ever burning about the corpse of the Queen'; and they went on foot, 'it being but little more than thirty miles'. It is an attractive fancy but it has the disadvantage that Arthur, Guinevere and Launcelot are not historical figures, though perhaps the events recorded did happen to people who were.

Rather similar was the experience of Miss Muriel Cobern in the summer of 1965 or 1966. She was walking back to the lay-by where she had left her car, at the top of White Horse Hill when, about fifty yards from the barrow on the hill, she felt very uneasy and noticed that it had become cold. Suddenly she could distinctly hear many horses' hooves thudding, as though a whole army was on the move. The whole hillside seemed to be alive with them, in full gallop, but not a horse was to be seen. She hurried on until she reached the long barrow known as Adam's Grave, when she found she could hear the hooves no longer.

History tells us that there was a great battle in AD 592 at a place called Wodensbeorge, which has been identified as Adam's Grave.

Miss Cobern also relates the story of a girl who in 1944-45 rode a pony from Marlborough to Avebury, returning home after dark. When she reached the Ridgeway at the top of Hackpen Hill the pony refused to go along it and, try as she would, it wouldn't budge. She had to turn round and return by road, a much longer way.

Several other ghost stories from the Downs tell of phenomena which caused reactions from animals without making any impression on humans. One concerned Harry Pinchin, a shepherd who lived for more than fifteen years in a lonely cottage on Martinsell Hill, near Wootton Rivers and on the edge of Savernake Forest. One night he was tending some sick lambs on the hill and heard the clock on Pewsey church strike midnight when, all of a sudden, all the ewes 'started hollerin', all three hundred of them'. The dog went mad with fear, 'the only time he had ever been scared of anything', and bolted away across the down, yelping. And yet Harry could hear nothing.

'I stood by the pens and listened, and all was quiet,' he said. 'I felt my hair and it were standing up straight under me cap.'

But he never had any idea what caused all the rumpus.

And then there was the lady who took friends to visit the churches of Alton Barnes and Alton Priors. They had visited the first and were on their way to the second, which they could see across the fields, when they took a short cut by way of a footpath. A small dog belonging to one of the friends took a violent objection to that footpath, making its mistress take a much longer route. On the return journey the lady picked up the dog to prevent a repetition of that nonsense but it struggled free and went off along the roundabout way, rejoining the party when they left the footpath.

Later enquiries revealed that the suspect path was a section of the Ridgeway.

A lady resident at All Cannings was riding her horse on the Downs near Tan Hill and the Wansdyke when the horse suddenly stopped, pricked up his ears and refused to go another step. Its rider urged it forward, whereupon it turned about and galloped back the way it had come.

And another All Cannings story. The owner of a Burmese cat says that it 'shows signs of great agitation' when it passes an ash tree at the top of Old Rectory Lane. Miss Kathleen Wiltshire adds that her terriers sometimes stop in the same place on their walks and refuse to go any further.

It is said that horses must never be turned out into a field at Allington, near Devizes; otherwise witches would ride them. Horses which ignored this prohibition were found in the morning with tangled manes and muddy sides and obviously very tired.

This is a classic witch story. I heard it many times as a boy in my native village of Pitton and I dare say it belongs, too, to half the villages of Wiltshire. It is actually a smuggling story, concocted to explain why horses were found in various stages of exhaustion, supposedly after a night in the stable. They had been requisitioned by smugglers to carry loads of contraband brandy by muddy tracks across country. Everyone knew about it but everyone kept quiet.

Nevertheless at Allington people say that the sound of horses' hooves is heard at night. And, what is more significant, a small dog belonging to a cottager once refused point-blank to accompany its mistress on a walk across that field, evidently seeing something that she could not.

The lords of the manor of Hill Deverill were the Coker family, the last of whom, Sir Henry Coker, died in 1730. Known as 'Old Coker', he is said to haunt the district, following his hounds in a ghostly hunt that takes in a round barrow, known as Gun's Church, on the Downs. The sound of galloping horses, huntsmen's horns blowing and chains rattling can at times be heard on stormy nights. Sometimes the phantom hunt even goes through the gardens of the manor-house.

And workmen winnowing corn one day in a down barn on Durnford Down were disturbed by the sound of galloping approaching through a flock of sheep grazing on the Downs. The sheep were panic-stricken, the barn doors were slammed shut, and the men heard the 'scrooping' sound of a leather saddle. Then the sounds died away, as though the horse had passed, and the sheep resumed their grazing.

One night the vicar of Heddington heard a great commotion on the Downs near his vicarage, as though there was a major traffic of men and horses. In the morning he phoned the police who, however, could offer no explanation. Nor were there any signs of activity on the ground.

A parallel instance occurred on the Downs (location unrecorded) of a hiker who decided to camp out on a downland hillside. When he had settled down for the night he heard, in the valley below, the sounds of marching feet and then the bustle and activity of men pitching camp. So in the morning he descended the hill to see who his neighbours were. There was no one there, nor any sign of a camp. Not a blade of grass had been trampled on.

A letter from a Mr T. Siree relates the story of a mystery house that is only partially solved. He writes:

> My parents had rented a cottage in Savernake for the summer. We had just come back from India, where we went during my first year of life. I was then eight years of age. The cottage had been rented through an adver-

tisement, and there was no connection between us and the locality. When we drove up I asked my parents why we were arriving at the back door, only to be told that the back door was on the other side, by the kitchen. I was puzzled, too, by the staircase, which I maintained was the servants' not 'our' stairs. It was pointed out that there was only one staircase in the cottage; I persisted that there was another staircase and lots more rooms. But there only stretched a blank wall, cutting off a shrubbery which grew right up to the house.

My mother found out that the cottage was indeed all that was left of a large coaching inn that had been burnt down some fifty years before. Only the servants' quarters had been saved, and no attempt had been made to rebuild the main part, as the need for so large a place had passed. So they built a wall across, cutting off the burnt-out building, which had been roughly levelled and allowed to form a shrubbery.

To this day I can draw the plan of the original house, which I know in detail, and which subsequently proved to be wholly accurate.

What can be the explanation of that?

And here is a similar instance, from about 1962.

A schoolgirl of about 12 took her dog for a walk on the Downs by the Wansdyke on Tan Hill. When she returned she asked who lived in a house she had seen. No one, not even the oldest shepherds who had spent their lives on the Downs, had any knowledge of a house there. They thought she was romancing. She insisted that she was not.

'It had a stable adjoining it,' she declared, 'with a horse looking out over the half-door, and chickens pecking about outside.'

She was so certain that she retraced her steps, looking for it, without success.

There is a sequel. A few years later Kathleen Wiltshire borrowed from the library a book containing some very old illustrations. One was a view of Tan Hill, which showed, in the very place where the girl had seen it, a house, just as she had described it. Two figures in smocks were standing nearby, testifying to the antiquity of the picture.

And here is another episode.

A visitor to Old Sarum in 1967 watched a boy swinging from the branch of an old yew tree growing on the outer earthworks. She took a second look at him and saw that he was dressed like a Saxon peasant, in a rough tunic with short cloak, both brown, and lighter-coloured leggings, criss-crossed with thongs at the knee. He wore sandals and had short, tousled hair. Her attention was distracted for an instant, and when she looked again he had vanished.

8   Black Dogs

Black dogs are apparently frequent companions to travellers on lonely tracks and lanes in Wiltshire. Kathleen Wiltshire has listed no fewer than forty-five of them, as follows:

1. On Doghill Barrow, due north of Stonehenge.
2. Near Wilbury House, Cholderton.
3. At midnight on a road near Lacock.
4. On a road near Melksham.
5. At a lonely spot between Wootton Rivers and Pewsey.
6. In Abingdon Park Lane, Cricklade.
7. On a road near Stourton.
8. At the dower house at Stourhead.
9. At Hinton Brook.
10. At Coate, near Bishops Cannings.
11. Between Horton and Coate.
12. Longbridge Deverill (Cow Down).
13. On a road near Crockerton.
14. At Chapmanslade, at a place called Black Dog Wood, near Black Dog Hill and Black Dog Farm.
15. By the church at Foxham.
16. Near Quemerford, Calne.
17. On a lane between Manton and Marlborough.
18. By a barrow on Roundway Down, Devizes.
19. The road between Hilmarton and Lyneham.

20. The road between Wootton Bassett and Lyneham, at a place known as Black Dog Cottages.
21. A lonely road known as Toothill, between Swindon and Wootton Bassett.
22. The road between Moredon and Haydon Wick, Swindon.
23. A lane in Donhead St Mary.
24. A Roman road in Wilton, Grafton.
25. A Roman site at Mildenhall.
26. A Roman road in Collingbourne Woods.
27. Maud Heath's Causeway, near Chippenham.
28. A chalkpit between Great Durnford and Netton.
29. The Long Barrow at West Kennett, 'at sunrise on the longest day'.
30. A huge megalithic tomb near the Bath Road by Fyfield.
31. By the gorge on the road between Ramsbury and Axford.
32. Between All Cannings and Allington.
33. Between All Cannings Cross and the village.
34. In the ghost story of Edward Avon.
35. On a footpath between Cadley and Marlborough.
36. A path at Urchfont.
37. The churchyard at Bishops Cannings.
38. A lane at Dauntsey.
39. There is a Black Dog Bridge at Minety.
40. The Talbot Inn at Ebbesbourne Wake has for its sign a black dog.
41. Back at All Cannings again, a track behind The Grange.
42. Between All Cannings and Stert.
43. The inn sign of a village near Donhead St Mary.
44. A black dog, accompanying a black monk, at Bradestoke Abbey, near Lyneham.
45. A bridge near Pewsey.

The majority of these consist of just a sighting, as of the

hound seen at times at Wilbury House, near Cholderton, which is described as resembling a black retriever. 'It is said to keep anyone company who crosses the driveway after dusk; it does not bark but pants as though it had been running.' It has been seen by several people at different times.

However, there are variations, one being of hounds with 'gurt eyes as big as saucers'. One used to sit on a stone-heap by a roadside at Coate, near Bishops Cannings, at about the turn of the century. It sat quietly enough, but if anyone picked up a stone to throw it its eyes grew larger and larger. And then there is the megalithic tomb or dolmen, known as the Devil's Den, on the Bath road less than two miles from Marlborough, which at midnight on certain dates the devil, with a yoke of four white oxen, tries in vain to move. The roofstone to which he harnesses the oxen weighs seventeen tons. While this operation is proceeding a huge white dog, 'with eyes like burning coals', watches from under the grave.

A large black dog 'with great blazing eyes as big as saucers' met a man walking from Calne to Coate to visit his grandfather, thought to be on his death-bed. He had got part of the way when this huge dog appeared. He picked up a stone and threw it at the animal, which immediately disappeared. As he drew near to Coate he met the local undertaker who told him that his grandfather had just passed away.

During the war a farmer near Pewsey received a telephone call late at night to say that his cattle were straying on to the highway. So he woke up his landgirl and together they set out to find the cows. At about midnight as they approached Cuckoo bridge they saw coming towards them across the bridge a lady dressed in black and leading a large dog on a sparkling chain. They stopped to let the lady cross the bridge, which she did ... and then she and the dog vanished. The watchers were near enough to hear the lady's skirts rustling.

A man once made a wager that he would ride from Wincanton market to his home in Stourton in seven minutes. In his attempt he was thrown from his horse while going at full gallop and broke his neck. And now, on New Year's Eve, his ghost appears, galloping along the lane where he fell and accompanied by a huge black dog. Curiously enough, the horseman is said to be headless!

A more mundane explanation suggests itself for a 'shaggy dog' who frightened the cart-horses and their carters when they went to bring them in from the pastures to their stable in the morning. This was at Hinton Brook and must have been in the summertime, when the horses were lying out. The carters declared that the horses came galloping home and stood there shivering, covered with lather.

That is a classic account of horses 'borrowed' by smugglers about their nefarious nocturnal business. The carters were doubtless bribed to shut their eyes and ears, and the villagers let it be understood that they were afraid to pass that way after dark.

On Palm Sunday the people of Longbridge Deverill walked up to Cow Down where, from time immemorial, they had held a picnic. But one Sunday a huge dog appeared and so frightened them that the festival was discontinued. One would like to know more of the circumstances.

In the same district a large black dog with bristling hair is to be seen on a certain road and on certain nights, breathing fire from its nostrils. And at Chapmanslade, only four miles away, a dog with burning eyes haunts a hillside road which passes the evocatively named Black Dog Wood. Old Coker, already mentioned, also belongs to the Deverill valley, and he has been identified with the Wild Hunt which can be heard galloping over the Downs on stormy nights, sounding his horn and with his hounds baying. The dog which appears to travellers by Black Dog Wood near Chapmanslade has an unsavoury reputation, for anyone who sees it 'will be dead by Christmas'.

The Wild Hunt is a common feature of northern mythologies. It is known by a variety of names – the Hounds of Hell, the Yeth Hounds, the Gabriel Hounds, the Seven Whistlers. In the Norse pantheon the leader of the Hunt was Woden, who careered across the stormy night sky followed by his pack of hounds in full cry. Yet long before the Norsemen raided and invaded the British Isles the Celts too had their dogs of hell (Annwn) who behaved in exactly the same manner. Later, as Christianity superseded the old religions, the Wild Hunt came to be regarded as a host of howling demons, pursuing the wicked and led by the devil. When the Huntsman became identified as the devil his prey consisted of Jews, unbaptized children and infidels, though any mortals who put themselves in his power by their misdeeds could also be his quarry.

A study of the numerous manifestations of the Hounds of Hell soon reveals that they are often heard but very seldom seen, and attempts to describe their wild calls suggest a probable identification with migrating birds of species that call or clamour in chorus as they fly high across the night sky; those which best match the descriptions are the wild goose, curlew, golden plover, whimbrel and wigeon.

In Norse mythology Woden has as his associates the Valkyries, those terrible battle-maidens who, by reading the omens in bloody entrails, decide on the persons to be slain in the forthcoming conflict. They are sometimes depicted as savage though beautiful creatures riding on wolves across the sky, while blood drips from the clouds. If Woden is the Huntsman, these would be his hounds.

If we were to probe back even further into prehistory we might find that the Valkyries were originally priestesses who selected victims for sacrifice and then slew them. It is a blood-stained track that we have ventured along.

There is an ancient practice of sacrificing a dog and burying it under the doorposts or walls of a new building, so that its spirit shall be a perpetual guard for the place. Another explanation of many black dog stories is that they were kept alive by mothers trying to keep their children from wandering into forbidden places. But a highly practical reason suggests that a dog with glaring eyes and jaws dripping saliva is an accurate description of a dog with rabies, which must have been a common sight in past centuries. Even now the howling of a dog is sometimes held to be a warning of an approaching death, which must once have been a fair conclusion if the dog was rabid.

A number of ghostly dogs from different parts of Wiltshire are said to drag a chain behind them. One which dragged with it a broken chain which rattled and clanked on the floor haunted a house, now demolished, in Preshute Lane, Marlborough. The most interesting feature of this apparition, however, is that it was headless! A dog which haunts the road known as Black Dog Cottages on the Wootton Bassett to Lyneham road has achieved the reputation that it is only seen by a person about to die!

Returning to Chapmanslade two stories are related which are out of the ordinary. A farmer's daughter was being courted by two men, neither of whom knew of the existence of the other. When they did discover what was happening they fought a duel, which resulted in one of them being killed. This man had a faithful dog who, seeing his master fall, immediately attacked his assailant and killed him. The farmer's daughter committed suicide and is buried at Dead Maid's Cross, at the top of Black Dog Hill. What happened to the dog is not recorded but presumably it too was killed, for its ghost now haunts Black Dog Hill.

The other story concerns a highwayman who used to hold up coaches on Black Dog Hill. He had trained his big black dog to jump on the coachman as he descended the steep hill, throwing everything into confusion during which the highwayman robbed the passengers. Eventually one coachman brought along a gunman who, when the dog attacked, shot it. Whereupon the dog became yet another ghost haunting the hill.

9 Witches

Wiltshire's best known witch is Lyddie Shears of Winterslow, who lived in the early years of the nineteenth century. Even at the beginning of the present century tales of Lyddie Shears used to be bandied about the markets, Romsey market in particular. It is said that she used to offer gipsy merchandise at the doors of cottages. Those who had the moral courage to refuse her blandishments would remain free of her evil influence, but those who had not, did her bidding.

An old man related how, in his young days, if they took Lyddie baccy and snuff she would go out with flint and steel striking sparks, which attracted hares so that the poachers could knock them over. The legend is that she so teased a certain Farmer Tanner by turning herself into a hare for him to course with his greyhounds that the farmer sought the advice of the rector of West Tytherley. The hare had a habit of always disappearing in her garden. The good man recommended that a bullet be made of a melted-down sixpenny piece. With it the farmer shot the elusive hare, and the witch was found dead in her cottage with a silver bullet in her heart!

Miss Edith Olivier was able to supply a few additional details. 'The hare was shot dead as it entered the garden,' she wrote. 'But afterwards, as they called at the cottage, they saw the body of Lydia Shears lying on the floor dead, and upon examination the silver bullet was found to have caused her death.'

A few moments' reflection will reveal what nonsense this is. How was it established that a silver bullet in the heart was the cause of death? Was a surgeon summoned to perform a post-mortem? No, the recognized method of killing a witch was to shoot her with a silver bullet. This was followed in the case of Lyddie Shears, and the old woman was subsequently found dead. Therefore the silver bullet must have killed her.

A somewhat similar instance comes from Wick, near Downton, where six farmers were one day shooting hares. A hare appeared at the entrance of a track called Bally Hag Lane, so called because a witch lived there in a cottage and used to gather herbs along the hedgerows. The farmers, all good shots, each loosed two barrels at the hare but failed to stop it. A rather wild young retriever chased the hare back to the garden hedge of the cottage but shortly afterwards returned with its tail between its legs. After that the old woman was not seen for some weeks, and when she reappeared she was very lame and had bandages on her hands and neck. One can see how a legend arose out of purely circumstantial evidence.

And from Tidcombe comes an almost identical tale to that of Lyddie Shears. A farm foreman shot at and wounded a hare. That same day an old woman suspected of being a witch was taken ill and died. That was accepted as proof that she was indeed a witch.

A very different story is told in the reminiscences of an old shepherd recorded by Miss Edith Olivier in her book *Moonrakings*. The name of the village is not given but it may have been Knook.

A carter was coming home one day with a load of wood when an old woman asked him to put her faggot on his waggon. As she had a reputation as a witch he refused. But when he tried to go on he found the horses could not move the waggon, though they tried even to breaking the harness. At last he was forced to unharness the horses and take them home, leaving the waggon where it was. His master was extremely angry but when he himself went to the scene the next day he too found that the waggon would not move. Until the witch's faggot was put on it that is, and then it moved straight away.

A strange story is told of a carter who, in about 1865, left Manor Farm, Wootton Rivers, soon after midnight with a waggon-load of corn to take to Devizes market. He had three horses to pull the waggon. He had not got far and was just negotiating a bend in the road when the leading horse dropped dead. The other two stood trembling and could not be induced to move. At last in despair he turned them round and made for home, the horses responding readily enough as soon as they were facing towards their stables.

In the morning the farmer went with his carter to look at the dead horse and could find no cause of death. But on its back was found a piece of thick straw, presumably a plait of sorts. This, said the know-alls, was what caused the death. The straw was a witch who had chosen to take this form, and if the carter had beaten the horse across the straw sufficient to draw blood her power would have been broken.

In one village, when anything went wrong on a certain farm the tenant used to send five shillings to the local witch, firmly believing that she was responsible. One poor woman, who had made several batches of heavy bread, put the blame on the witch and paid her a fee, asking her to break the spell. This the witch did by burning a piece of heavy dough in the fire, but something went wrong for when the dough caught fire so did the witch's cap!

In another village, unidentified, lived an old woman who was said by certain villagers to be a witch. Boys used to taunt her as she walked down the village street, and one day a particularly bold and naughty boy threw a stone which grazed the old woman's cheek. She stopped, pointed at him with her finger and said,

'You throwed thik stone! You don't spake again till I say!'

From that moment the boy was struck dumb, or

appeared to be, and this went on for some time until his mother called in the rector. He arranged a meeting in his study, at which the mother volubly accused the old woman of causing his dumbness. The old woman turned her back on her with contempt and said to the boy,

'Spake, boy! You can spake as well as I can, cain't ee?'

'Yes,' said the boy.

Where the counties of Wiltshire and Somerset meet there once lived a witch who was greatly feared for her interference with the activities of the villagers, such as butter-making, causing unseasonable storms and producing swarms of fleas. In the end they went in a body to the witch's cottage, bent on mischief. She saw them coming and proceeded to escape by way of the huge old-fashioned chimney, the conventional mode of exit for a witch. In her haste, however, her shift caught fire, so she quickly removed it and threw it down, flaming, on the crowd of women. And thereupon she disappeared, never to be seen again!

About 150 years ago the curate of Allington, near Amesbury, had had a convivial evening with some friends but, on attempting to mount his horse, fell and broke his neck. His companions were so terrified that they carried the body to a field a few hundred yards away and dropped it down a well.

Following this incident the horses in a neighbouring stable became very restless every evening and often broke loose. After a time, one of the carters who slept in the stable could endure it no longer and, remarking to his companion that he would 'settle it', climbed into the loft.

In a few moments he came tumbling down again, looking ghastly. Nothing could ever induce him to say what he had seen, but the horses were never so troublesome again.

Many years later the woman at whose house the curate and his friends had been carousing, feeling her end was near, sent for a neighbour and started to tell him what had really happened that night. She had hardly started, though, when she was seized with violent pains and couldn't proceed. So her secret died with her.

On Winklebury Hill, overlooking the village of Berwick St John where the little River Chalke has its headwaters, at certain seasons they hold a witches' festival. It is ostensibly centred on a thorn bush, which is the descendant of a previous one known as the Witches' Scrag Tree, but the whole hill is reckoned to be a haunt of witches. They are said to have become entangled in the thorny branches as they rode low over the hill on their broomsticks by the light of the full moon. The hillside was littered with their corpses.

I believe it is the local Women's Institute which has revived the festival. I once asked a participant whether they ever saw any witches nowadays.

'Well, not exactly,' she confessed, 'but they are all disguised as thorn bushes, and there are plenty of those. After all, witches can disguise themselves as anything.'

In spite of its secret character, the Society of the Horseman's Word (see p.120) acted as a safeguard against witches, who had the ability, unless checked, to transform men into horses in order to provide themselves with steeds, completing their wicked work by having them shod by the devil. Horses are reputed to have psychic powers and to be able to see ghosts, which is borne out by some of the incidents related earlier. On seeing a piebald horse, spit and wish, but take care not to make your wish known. And do not look at its tail. Horses are particularly susceptible to the Evil Eye, to protect them from which horse brasses were first devised.

A carter on a Pewsey farm told Kathleen Wiltshire that a witch riding on a horse would clutch the mane and the tail and that was why horses were docked. Some horses had their manes and tails plaited with straw in thirteen braids, to which a tuft of red wool was sometimes added.

Associated with witchcraft is the Ooser, a fearsome character bearing many of the elements of the bogey-man. The Ooser is usually reckoned to belong to Dorset but he was known in Wiltshire as well. When I was a child engaging in some form of horseplay my father would endeavour to quieten me by saying, 'Now that's enough, 'r the Ooser'll have ee.' This was in the village of Pitton, well within Wiltshire.

The last traditional Ooser vanished from its home in Melbury Osmond, in West Dorset, about the turn of the century, but in recent years one or two have been resurrected. Fortunately photographs of the Melbury Osmond Ooser have survived, so it has been possible to fashion fairly exact replicas.

The Ooser mask was worn by a tireless character who capered about in the processions in village festivals, doing his best to scare people. The mask had huge, staring eyes, a mouth with a set of gleaming teeth, the lower jaw of which could be worked by a string, a great topknot of black hair, fuzzy whiskers and, most important of all, an imposing set of bull's horns.

He was, in fact, a representation of the old horned god, who was also personified in the aurochs, the wild bull, of the forest. He was a god of fertility and was, in particular, associated with May Day revels.

In Dorset the Ooser has close associations with that remarkable hill carving, the Cerne Abbas Giant. For many centuries, until quite recent times, the people of Cerne used to erect a tall maypole during the night before May Day, in the Frying Pan earthwork which occupies a hillcrest site just above the Giant. In the morning they would decorate the maypole and dance around it, a revel in which I remember participating less than twenty years ago. The Ooser, standing an impressive eight feet tall and appearing even larger in the morning mist, took a lead in the proceedings.

I am intrigued by the resemblance to the Ooser of the

Salisbury Giant, who parades the streets of Salisbury on royal occasions, such as coronations and jubilees. He stands about twelve feet high and has a swarthy complexion, a bushy black beard and huge staring eyes. Very similar, in fact, to the Ooser. He is carried by a bearer hidden beneath full medieval robes, and records of the Middle Ages refer to him as St Christopher. Jean Morrison suggests that he may well belong to an earlier tradition, and to my mind he looks exactly like the old bull god.

Jean Morrison writes:

At some time during the Middle Ages he was appropriated by the Tailors' Guild, whose patronal festival fell on June 24, Midsummer Day. We do not know how old he is but he went in the procession led by the Mayor and Corporation to meet Henry VII and his Queen in 1496, and he was old then. He was an important figure in all celebrations, particularly St John's (Midsummer) Night, St Osmund's Night (July 16) and St Peter's Night (August 1), all summer festivals, when he was accompanied by the Hobnob, his esquires bearing mace, sword and lantern, the Morris dancers, three black boys and a devil ...'

In the nineteenth century the Giant and Hobnob made frequent appearances in Salisbury, and Jean Morrison suggests that they were not always especially stately or decorous:

... while the bearers of the Giant refreshed themselves (in a pub) the Morris dancers became the centre of attraction, dancing to traditional tunes, three dressed as men in streamers and bells, and three as women, and one as a fool. Then, when the collecting box had gone round, and thirst was satisfied, the procession continued on its way, perhaps a little less steadily. And all the way the two flautists played old tunes, which were half-drowned by the heavy thud of the drum representing the sound of the Giant's footsteps, and the Hobnob rushed about, jaws snapping, chasing the girls and making them squeal with pretended fright, his bearer's blackened face, half-hidden under helmet and veil, adding to the terrifying appearance of the black horse.

I well remember marching, as a schoolboy, in procession behind the Giant and hearing that sombre thudding of the drum.

10 Witchcraft Accessories

We have already noted some of the more spectacular beasts that haunt the Wiltshire countryside. Black dogs are particularly frequent, and there are spectral pigs, donkeys, horses and other creatures. The pig was a sacred animal in the Celtic religion, and it is at least possible that some legends of exciting boar hunts have their origins in the ceremonial hunting and killing of a pig-god.

Consider, for instance, the story of Sir Richard Grobham, who was steward to Sir Thomas Gorges, of Longford Castle, at the time of Queen Elizabeth I. He lived at the manor of Wishford and is noted as a great hunter, for he slew a wild boar in Groveley Woods which had terrorized the district. The tree under which the boar received its mortal wound was called Boar's Tree, but after it was stabbed it managed to flounder across the river. It eventually collapsed and died in a meadow on the farther side. And from that time onwards, the owner of the Boar's Tree could claim a pook of hay from the meadow where the boar died. In 1857, more than two hundred years after the event, men were still living who had exercised that right. Sir Richard's sword and helmet were hung in Wishford church, where Sir Richard Colt Hoare saw them at the beginning of the nineteenth century.

It is impossible at this stage to disentangle the various threads of which this story is composed, but it looks like an historical incident used to explain a much more ancient custom.

In later times pigs were credited with psychic powers and with being able to see the wind, which last is still widely half-believed. A meal of pig's brains will force a person to speak the truth. If a pig dies of disease it has to be buried trotters uppermost to prevent an epidemic from developing. A dried pig's bladder cut open, smeared with goose fat and worn as a chest protector is said to ward off ague. Or you can carry a dried pig's tail in your pocket.

Much of the severe ill-treatment meted out to cats in past centuries was due to the belief that they were really witches in disguise. Until recently some people were very careful about what they said when a cat was present, in case the animal turned back into human shape and repeated what it had heard.

Cats were, and probably still are, credited with psychic powers. They are said to have foreknowledge of approaching disasters. When a cat deserts a house where a person is lying sick, that person will shortly die, as happened once fairly recently in my experience. When in the Fen country cats go upstairs to sleep, a flood is imminent – and there are many instances to confirm the accuracy of this belief.

Cats are said to be effective killers of adders, and the prejudice against May kittens (superficially nonsensical) is perhaps due to the fear that by late summer, when adders are numerous, they would bring adders into the house. There is a belief that May kittens prefer snakes to mice and rats, which they will ignore. An old book advises, 'You should drown a May kitten; it is unlucky to keep it.'

Cats are said to be fond of ghosts and to purr whenever they meet one. They can predict a high wind by clawing at curtains and carpets; and rain is certain when you observe a cat busily washing behind its ears. If a cat sneezes near a bride on her wedding morning, it forecasts a lucky and happy marriage for her.

Hares, like cats, were called 'pusses', and some country stories revolve around amusing errors that have arisen through confusion of the two. My father used to tell one about an acquisitive resident who saw a well-known poacher apparently stalking a hare across some distant fields. Later he met the man who was carrying something in a sack. He asked what was in the sack and was told, 'A puss, of course!'

He offered half-a-crown for it; then asked to be allowed to see it.

'What! Here in the middle of the village street?' exclaimed the poacher, and the buyer saw the force of the argument. So he paid his half-crown and took the bag home. Inside was a ginger cat.

We have already dealt extensively with dogs, especially spectral ones. Dogs are commonly supposed to be able to see ghosts and to have advance warning of death. A spayed bitch is said to be an effective protection against ghosts and demons. In some places black dogs have been buried on the north side of churches, where the Devil's Door is to be found, to keep the devil out.

So great was our ancestors' fear of rabies that any dog who bit a person was doomed. It was believed that if ever, in the future, the dog became mad its victim, though of years previously, would go mad too. Another precaution was to take some hair from the dog, fry it and place it on the wound with a sprig of rosemary. Hence the saying, 'The hair of the dog that bit you.'

Horses, too, have featured quite extensively in this book, so perhaps it is sufficient to remind ourselves that they were sacred animals in the ancient Celtic religion. The Celts had a goddess, Epona, who sometimes took the form of a mare, and they also believed that the souls of the dead travelled on horseback to Paradise. Like dogs, horses are said to be psychic and to be able to see ghosts, including the ghosts of people not yet dead. This sensitivity is said to make horses particularly vulnerable to the Evil Eye.

Horses with four white feet are widely regarded as

being unlucky, though two white feet bring good luck. In some versions it is white horses that are lucky, but on meeting one you should cross your fingers and spit.

The technique of controlling horses, making them stand motionless despite all attempts to make them move until they were 'released by whoever cast the spell on them', makes interesting reading. It was practised by a Toadman, who had been duly initiated by secret rites.

The novice had to catch a live toad and peg it to an ant-heap until the ants had eaten the bones clean. Alternatively the toad could be thrown to the ground with sufficient force to kill it. The bones were then carried in the pocket until they were thoroughly dry. On the night of a full moon the man had to go down to a stream and throw in the bones, which were said to scream horribly in the process. One bone would detach itself from the rest and start to move upstream. This one had to be rescued by the Toadman, who thus achieved his magic power. According to one version, however, the devil appeared as the bone was retrieved from the water.

There was a standard demonstration of the Toadman's power over horses. An ordinary garden fork was stuck into a heap of straw and one or two powerful horses were hitched to it. Try as they would, they could not shift it. When the Toadman gave the word or sign, however, one horse could move it easily.

Bad luck will attend a woman who is present when a mare is giving birth to a foal. And a mare in foal must never be harnessed to a waggon which was being used to draw a coffin to the church, for the death of the mare, or her foal, would assuredly follow. Old-time carters would keep a brown paper parcel of clipped yew from a female tree under their bed for a year or more, before adding a little to the horse's rations to make his coat shine or generally improve its appearance. Chopped walnut leaves were reputed to be good for worming horses. Marchwort in the drinking water of horses was said to keep the animals healthy, but the herb had to be picked with the left hand only, without looking back. Sores on horses could be cured by gathering red thistles before daybreak and putting one on each of the four corners of a compass, with a stone in the middle.

A mixture of oil of origanum, oil of rosemary, oil of cinnamon and oil of fennel was said to be effective in controlling an unruly animal. It was given to the horse on lumps of sugar and was also used in stopping a horse and forcing it to remain immobile. A hand covered with milk and vinegar acted as an antidote.

It is extremely unlucky for a hare to cross one's path when starting on a journey; better to turn round and wait until next day. And so strong was the belief that hares and witches were interchangeable that some countrymen (and women) refused to eat a hare, lest they commit cannibalism. A hare running down a village street was said to forecast a fire. The hare was another sacred animal in the Celtic pantheon.

A black cock was said to be clairvoyant and could warn of the approach of danger. A cock crowing by a house door indicated that a stranger could be expected, but a cock crowing at midnight heralded a death. Cocks were frequent sacrificial victims and were often buried under the foundations of houses, as a protection against evil spirits. On Candlemas Day, which is the Celtic festival of Imbolc, the ritual sometimes included the burial of a living cock at a place where three streams met.

Foxes were animals into which witches quite frequently transformed themselves. The belief that a fox's bite is poisonous seems to have been widespread. The poison could even be transmitted to anything the animal had bitten; hence it was dangerous to eat a hen killed by a fox. The belief is rendered plausible by the fact that foxes are susceptible to rabies. Stranger is the belief that a vixen cannot breed until her mother is dead.

When I was a boy enjoying the lurid light that bathes

the countryside after a thunderstorm my mother would exclaim,

'Oh, look! The fox's wedding!'

And she explained that that was the name given to that particular combination of dark, receding clouds and approaching bright sunbeams. It seemed a fanciful name, and I thought that my aunt's version – that it was really a corruption of 'the folkses' wedding', meaning the little folk or fairies – was likely enough to be correct.

Since then, however, I have come across the use of the term to explain exactly the same phenomenon in countries as far apart as Japan, Greece, Morocco and Bangladesh. The Japanese even specify the participants in the wedding; they say it is the fox marrying the wolf. To find such unanimity concerning an unusual and uncommon set of circumstances in such a wide variety of countries is a most remarkable piece of folklore.

The usual rhyme concerning the number of magpies seen together is:

One for sorrow;
Two for mirth;
Three for a wedding;
Four for a birth.

An alternative version runs:

One for sorrow, two for joy,
Three for marriage, four for a boy.
Six for silver, seven for gold,
Eight for a secret that's never been told.

One tale was that the magpie wouldn't go into the ark with Noah, preferring to stay outside and jabber exultantly over the drowning world. For this reason the magpie is an unlucky bird, whose chatter can herald disaster, though that can be averted by spitting at it. It is also a wise precaution to doff one's hat when meeting a magpie, or always to carry an onion in one's pocket. A magpie is such an evil bird that in Scotland it was said to carry a drop of the devil's blood hidden under its tongue, and for a magpie to alight on a roof presaged the death of one of the inhabitants. But against that a magpie alighting on a roof was a sign that the roof was sound.

The raven is now virtually extinct in much of Britain, so all its lore must be given in the past tense. They were a favourite witches' bird, much used by them on their nefarious business and were the supernatural guardians of buried treasure. They were also protective of human beings, especially good ones (as in the Biblical story of Elijah), but would betray the hiding-place of evil-doers. A baby would die if anyone stole eggs from a raven's nest.

The hooting of an owl is an omen of death, especially if heard near a house. For centuries owls were so feared, being regarded as witches, that they were killed whenever possible, and some people were so scared of them that they refused to touch a dead one. But an owl nailed to a barn door was said to be a protection against evil spirits.

For a shrew to run over one's foot was exceptional bad luck, a mishap which could happen to a person sitting quietly on grass. By running over a cow while it was lying down it could cause the milk yield to dry up. The remedy was to bore a hole in the trunk of an ash tree, put a live shrew in it, and seal it. Shrew ashes used to be common features of the countryside, and it was a common practice to set aside an ash tree in a parish for use again and again.

Snakes naturally feature prominently in witch lore. Witches are said to have been able to extract the fangs of adders and to use them medicinally. Perhaps they were indeed able to do so. One remedy for a snake's bite was to rub the wound with the dried head of a snake. An adder stone, formed from the skins of snakes, was used to rub the eyes to cure cataracts. Exactly what serpent's eggs or snakestones were no one knows, though most people think they were a type of fossil. Country folk used to say that they were formed by a snake breathing on a hazel wand. They used them for curing snakebites.

A curious belief, still held, is that an adder, no matter how badly wounded, cannot die until the sun has set.

Toads were frequently kept as pets or familiars by witches, but there is a curious ambiguity about them, for in some districts they are considered very lucky. At Wherwell, just over the border in Hampshire, in a dungeon beneath the priory a duck once laid an egg which was hatched by a toad and produced a cockatrice. It grew into a fearsome monster and was eventually slain by a man who persuaded it to batter itself into near exhaustion by fighting its reflection in a mirror. The Romans believed that when a dagger blade was placed on a toad's back the creature would turn around slowly until the dagger was pointing due north – and then stop.

One of the strangest customs associated with bird lore is the Hunting of the Wren, which traditionally took place on Boxing Day. The hunt was conducted with much ceremony by men adorned with coloured ribbons and bearing with them a kind of hobby-horse. It dates back to Neolithic times, and the probability is that the wren became associated with ideas of the underworld because of its habit of creeping into crevices of rocks and caves and perhaps of tombs constructed of great stones. As such it could logically be identified with the powers of darkness, at the time of the winter solstice when all life and vegetation seemed to be threatened. The wren represented the champion of darkness, who was slain and by whose death the world was restored to life.

Oddly enough, for the rest of the year the wren was regarded with some respect, even affection.

The robin and the wren
Are God's cock and hen,

summarized the friendly esteem in which the robin is generally held. Its popularity is alleged to be due to a robin which tried to peck the nails from Christ's hands as he hung on the cross, reddening its breast with his blood. Anyone who stole a robin's egg would have his little finger grow crooked, and anyone who killed a robin would have his house burnt down. But for a robin to enter a house or even to tap at a window was considered very unlucky, even a herald of death, though in some districts an exception is made in the month of November!

The dove is another bird with which folklore deals kindly. It brings good luck, but must never be sold for cash or the chain of good fortune will be broken.

On the whole, the cuckoo is a lucky bird, though if it is heard calling after Old Midsummer Day (3 July) it heralds a death. Money should be turned in your pocket when the first is heard, and you can make a wish, but on no account look at the ground. If the first cuckoo calls twelve times, the coming year will be prosperous, and a child born when the first cuckoo of the year is calling will have a lucky life. But if you hear the first cuckoo when lying in bed it is a sign of illness or death, and it is also unlucky to hear it while fasting.

In former times cuckoos were supposed to turn into hawks in winter or to spend the winter months in fairy hills.

Bats were another creature into which witches quite frequently turned themselves. A bat flying three times around a house was a sure sign of the death of one of the inhabitants.

Spiders are generally omens of good luck, especially the little money spiders; put it in your pocket if one alights on you. A sufferer from ague should catch a spider and shut it in a box; as it expires the malady will die away. 'If you wish to live and thrive, let a spider run alive.'

11 A Witch's Herbal

According to old-time herbalists there are twelve mystic herbs, which are rosemary, sage, lavender, comfrey, rue, hellebore, wormwood, verbena, marjoram, vervain, mint and camomile. Nearly all plants, however, had magical properties and were therefore regarded with awe and respect.

Apple – In ancient religions the apple was highly prized and accepted as an emblem of the renewal of youth. The tree in the Garden of Eden is often stated to have been an apple, though there is no scriptural authority for it. Some believe that, as mistletoe is seldom found growing on oak, the Druidic ritual of gathering mistletoe from oak really refers to the apple. It was considered unlucky to cut down an apple tree, an attitude that can doubtless be traced back to the fact that both Roman and Celtic law imposed stiff penalties for the offence.

Many apple trees bear a few sprays of blossom in autumn, when the tree is bearing ripe apples, and to pick such a spray presages a death in the house.

Angelica – A strong protection against witchcraft. An infusion was used to relieve digestive troubles, especially flatulence; a mixture of angelica, peppermint and balm, in equal proportions, was taken hot before going to bed to relieve sore throats and promote sleep.

Arum Lily, or Cuckoo Pint – A suspect plant, perhaps due to the fact that it was supposed to have been introduced by nuns from Normandy. It was thought to give consumption (tuberculosis) to anyone who went near it if it were introduced to the house.

When corn was harvested by sickle the blade was, after being sharpened on the grindstone, rubbed over with an arum flower. This was thought to ensure that the cutting edge would remain sharp until harvest was over.

Ash – The old remedy for curing a hernia or rupture by passing the affected child through a split ash is based on sympathetic medicine. The ash must be a 'ground ash', that is, a sapling from a seedling that has never been cut. It must be split open for the length of two or three feet, the two sides of the gash levered open, and the naked child passed through, from east to west. The ritual must take place when dew is on the grass and must be undertaken by a girl and a boy; the child is handed through the ash by the girl and received by the boy. In some versions, the child has to be passed through three times. The ash sapling is then bound together, and as it heals so will the child. The remedy was also employed for rickets and a number of other ailments. (See also under Shrew p. 99).

A custom of probable Norse origin is the burning of the Ashen Faggot at Yuletide. Bound with withies, the faggot is placed on the hearth, and predictions are made according to how the bonds snap. In some districts ash keys and ash twigs are used as charms, and ash sticks are a protection against witches. A cure for toothache is to cut your toe-nails while sitting under an ash tree.

Betony – 'Sell your coat and buy betony' is an old Wiltshire saying illustrating the high regard in which this herb was held. It is effective in healing wounds, particularly burns.

Beans – Anyone meeting a witch can render her evil spells ineffective by spitting a bean at her. This may have been associated with the ancient belief that ghosts and spirits live in bean-fields. To fall asleep in a bean-field is to risk going mad, and if a pregnant mother eats beans her child may be mentally affected.

Birch – To protect horses from being ridden by witches on May Day, prop a birch tree decorated with red and white rags against the stable door.

For a couple to 'jump over a besom' together was at one time considered tantamount to being legally married, especially among itinerant peoples, such as pedlars, tinkers and navvies. If an unmarried girl inadvertently walked over a birch besom, or even over some birch branches, that was considered a sign that she would be a mother before a wife. Of course, witches were alleged to ride through the night sky on birch brooms.

Black Bryony – Steeped in gin, the berries and roots were a popular cure for chilblains. They were also used as a plaster for the relief of rheumatism and gout. The big root, scraped and moistened, was added to a horse's rations to help the animal's condition and cause its coat to shine, though there was a caution against using too much.

Red-berried Bryony – This plant is rare in Britain, but there are many legends and superstitions attached to it in the Mediterranean world. Its common name is the mandrake, and it has a large, deep, fleshy root which is almost invariably forked about two-thirds of the way down, giving it a fanciful resemblance to a human trunk. Because of its appearance there arose a belief that it was inhabited by a demon who would shriek horribly if an attempt were made to uproot it. Anyone who heard the ghastly sound would drop dead.

Bramble – The bramble was a sacred plant in the Celtic religion, on a par with the rowan and the oak. Sacred fires were fuelled by these three woods.

A former cure for whooping-cough was to crawl under a bramble that had formed a natural arch, the tip sending down a new root. Various refinements were introduced. In some instances the sufferer had to repeat the process nine times, usually on nine consecutive days (when the ailment would be getting better anyway!). Sometimes the bramble arch had to be on a parish boundary, and sometimes the patient had to be eating bread-and-butter during the exercise. Afterwards the bread-and-butter had to be given to a bird, who presumably took the disease and died.

The bramble was also effective in healing scalds. Nine bramble leaves were dipped in clear spring water and applied, one by one, to the wound. The following rhyme was repeated three times for each leaf:

Three ladies came from the east,
One brought fire, two brought frost,
Out with fire, and in with frost,
In the name of the Father and of the Son and of the Holy Ghost

Followed by three amens.

Camomile – Was used medicinally. For fractious children camomile flowers, picked when the sun was shining, were dried in the sun and kept in a close stoppered jar until required for use. A draught consisted of ten heads of camomile in a pint of barley water and sweetened with a large tablespoonful of honey. This was given hot at bedtime, and it could be repeated cold during the day. For earache, a bag of flannel was filled with camomile heads, warmed over the fire and held over the aching ear. It was also good for toothache and any pain in the neck. Camomile tea was a cure for biliousness.

Clover – In folklore clover and shamrock are often confused. They are supposed to bring good luck but in an earlier age the luck took specific forms, notably the gift of second sight, the power to detect witches and to see fairies.

Chicory – Was supposed to make the bearer invisible. Also it conveyed the power to open locked chests, by using a golden knife while holding a chicory leaf against the lock. But this could only be done on St James's Day (25

July), and the man had to work in total silence. If he spoke he died.

Cowslip – An ointment made by simmering cowslip heads in hog's lard, strained and then simmered with fresh flowers twice more was said to ease backache and to be good for freckles, spots and sunburn.

Daisy – A remedy for colds and coughs. Put the flowers in a jar, pour boiling water on them, cover tightly and allow to stand for twelve hours.

It is lucky to step on the first daisy of spring, and when you can stand on nine at once spring has truly arrived. But beware the dangers of uprooting a daisy, for the children of the family will grow up stunted. To know when she would marry, a girl had to pick a bunch of daisies with her eyes shut. Then she had to count the number of flowers, and that would tell her how many years she would have to wait.

Devil's-bit Scabious – This is said to be so efficacious at curing all human ailments that the devil bit off the end of the root, lest it should banish pain and illness altogether.

Elder – Was a sacred tree in the old Celtic religion and therefore a witch's tree. Some superstitions identify it as a benevolent plant while others say the reverse. Christian apologists identified it as the wood of which Christ's cross was made and also the tree from which Judas Iscariot hanged himself.

Because of its associations with the old religion no one would ever fall asleep under an elder tree, for fear of putting himself in the power of witches; it was even dangerous to venture near an elder after dark. Tales are told of how the cutting of an elder tree caused wounds on the limbs of witches, the inference being that the witch at the time had been living in the form of the tree. An elder tree cut on Midsummer Day would shed real blood. It is still considered unlucky to burn elder indoors on a fire, and many householders refuse to have it in the house. Elder flowers were barred from being taken indoors as they were thought to attract snakes. And the log which a witch left in her bed, adorned with her nightcap, to deceive inquisitive neighbours when she was absent on her nocturnal missions, was of elder.

Elm – Elm does not figure prominently in folklore at all. Such instances as do occur derive exclusively from confusion of names and the assumption that wych elm (which is a variety of elm) means 'witches' elm'. In fact, it is derived from an Anglo-Saxon word meaning to bend, but that does not prevent place names such as Witchford and Picketty Witch being spelt that way. They originated with the wych elm, Picketty Witch meaning the 'picked or three-cornered field where the wych elm stands'!

In some parts of the country a few twigs of wych elm are put into the butter barrel when the butter won't set.

Fern Seed – By analogy, the spores of ferns, or fern seed, which are so small as to be practically invisible, could confer on the gatherer the gift of invisibility. To be effective, however, the seed had to be gathered at midnight on Midsummer Eve by shaking the fronds over pewter plates. The exercise was viewed with disfavour by the devil who, by sending wind or rain or by using other tricks, tried to thwart the gatherers.

If, on the same night, a girl ran three times around the church while the clock was striking midnight, scattering the seed as she ran (or if she had been gathering fern seed at midnight, scattering it on her way home, half an hour later) she would see, by glancing over her shoulder, her future husband mowing the phantom crop of ferns with a scythe.

Foxglove – One of the ingredients used in the preparation of the ointment which gave witches the power to fly. It featured in a number of harmless concoctions which gave some relief to the ailments of our ancestors.

Groundsel – The presence of this common weed in a garden was associated with witchcraft. A large patch of it marked a spot where witches assembled; a small patch the place where a witch had urinated. Groundsel was a favourite plant of the devil, who would admit to his presence only those who brought him a posy of it; therefore a witch could not die in winter, when there were no groundsel flowers for her to gather. A patch of it, growing on a thatched roof, indicated that a witch had landed on or taken off from the roof.

Hawthorn – Hawthorn is a benevolent tree. Twigs of it hanging from or placed upon rafters gave protection against witches and lightning, while twigs of it hanging outside a cowshed ensured a good milk yield. The hawthorn is an emblem of hope, associated with the advent of spring and with festivities and rejoicing. The maypole around which young people danced on May Day was generally of hawthorn, and the foliage was often used for the wreath that adorned the Green Man. Flowering branches of hawthorn were carried by girls in wedding processions; but hawthorn was also used by witches, who rode upon broomsticks made of hawthorn.

Hazel – Forked hazel wands are widely employed by water-diviners, and in the past were also used to search for buried treasure and to point out thieves. To be most effective they must be cut on St John's Eve. In a number of instances burials dating from the Dark Ages have had crossed hazel wands placed on the breast of the corpse. Farther back, hazel wands seem to have been associated with the idea that a white serpent with mystical powers lived at the roots of a hazel tree. Hazel nuts were often used in divination.

Hemp – Hemp seed was widely used in divination. At midsummer and Hallowe'en a girl would sow hemp seed as she ran three times round the church while the clock was striking midnight. As she ran she recited:

Hemp seed I sow,
Hemp seed I hoe,

Hoping my true love will come after me and mow.

Then, looking over her shoulder, she would see the wraith of her lover following her with a scythe, or, according to some versions, raking the seed into a winding-sheet.

Hemp was widely believed to be the devil's flower, and it is worth remembering that the scientific name for it is Cannabis. Young women were not allowed to work in hemp-fields for fear that they would become barren; older women were affected by a severe rash on their arms; and harvesting the crop gave the workers severe headaches. Smoking the dried leaves had a stupefying effect.

Henbane – Was widely used by witches. In the form of 'twilight sleep' it brought relief to women in childbirth.

Holly – Holly trees left standing in a neatly-trimmed hedge, still a familiar sight in the countryside, are an indication that old witchcraft lore still lingers, though probably not now recognized as such. Holly was a witch tree, and it was considered very unlucky to cut it. Holly also makes a good hedge, not only to keep stock out or in but also as a protection against witches. For the same reason holly was a favourite wood for thresholds; no witch could cross it. A man setting out on a lonely journey at night felt safer if he carried a holly stick with him. It was also a protection against fire, lightning and sundry ailments.

Holly was a sacred tree before the Christian era, and, although its exact significance is unknown, its acceptance by Christians was not entirely wholehearted. Although tolerated in churches, it must not be brought in until Christmas Eve or allowed to remain after Twelfth Night, a taboo often extended to houses. Cows thrived if a sprig of Christmas holly was placed in the cowshed.

Honeysuckle – A wedding would shortly follow if honeysuckle were brought indoors. Its scent was supposed to inspire erotic dreams in girls.

Hyssop – A handful of dried hyssop in a linen cloth immersed in boiling water was effective in treating a black or bloodshot eye. It was also a protection against the Evil Eye.

Ivy – Ivy was considered an unlucky plant to bring into the house, even a small piece of ivy clinging to a log. But cups made of ivy wood were said to have curative properties. To drink from them would cure whooping-cough or sober up a drunken man. Ivy was also used widely in a variety of medical concoctions.

Juniper – Juniper smoke drives away cattle plague as well as witches and evil spirits. A sprig of juniper stuck in a cow's tail has the same effect. A juniper bush growing near a house brings good fortune, and to dream of juniper berries heralds an important achievement, though to dream of a juniper bush is unlucky.

Marsh-mallow – The sap of marsh-mallow was used in the preparation of an ointment smeared liberally over the hands of a person undergoing the ordeal of trial by fire in medieval times. It enabled him to hold red-hot iron without coming to any harm.

Mistletoe – Mistletoe has magical properties. Hung on a house wall, it will protect the house against lightning. A slip of mistletoe cut with a new dagger on Hallowe'en after the gatherer has walked three times sunwise around the tree is a charm against witchcraft and injury in battle.

In the old Celtic religion mistletoe growing on a sacred oak – a rare occurrence – was cut with great ceremony by a Druid with a golden sickle and caught by another Druid in a white apron before it could touch the ground, after which two white bulls were sacrificed. The soul of the oak was believed to be present in the mistletoe, which lived in winter when the tree itself appeared to be dead. One of the main purposes of the Druidical ceremony was to promote the fertility of the earth and the growing of good crops; the custom of kissing under the mistletoe presumably derives from this.

Mugwort – Under the roots of the mugwort are found what appear to be nodules of coal. They are, in fact, a decayed part of the root, but they have long been considered to possess powerful magical properties. In particular, if dug up at midnight on Midsummer Eve and placed under a pillow they will help a girl dream of her future husband.

This was one of the plants hung over a house door on Midsummer Eve to frighten away witches and the devil. It also protected the house against lightning. If mugwort were laid under the door it prevented couples from quarrelling. And it was believed that the leaves always turned towards the north.

Nightshade – There are four British species of nightshade – woody nightshade, black nightshade, deadly nightshade and henbane. The two last are the most toxic and were used extensively in witches' brews and potions. Belladonna, well known as an hallucinatory drug, is derived from deadly nightshade and was probably used by soothsayers to induce second sight. Witches valued it because from it they could make an ointment which, if rubbed over their bodies, enabled them to fly.

Oak – Much magic is attached to the oak. Every carpenter knows that wooden pegs rather than nails should be used with oak, but less well known is the belief that a nail driven into an oak trunk is supposed to be a cure for toothache. Oak is a protection against lightning but not for the wicked man.

Many May Day customs were associated with the oak. The Green Man, or Jack-in-the-Green, was garlanded and disguised in oak sprays. Oak branches are still cut and brought in triumph to decorate village houses and churches. From Wishford oak boughs are taken to Salisbury Cathedral on Oak Apple Day and there ceremonially presented to the Dean before the high altar.

The Celtic religion was intimately bound up with the oak, its worship being frequently conducted in oak groves, its priests garlanded with oak leaves. Among northern peoples the woodpecker was held in reverence because its drumming resembled the sound of thunder amid oak trees. They also revered sacred fires, which were kept burning perpetually with oak wood. In early times oak trees were probably identified with the spirit of a god-king. When the time came for him to be ritually slain, the tree would be felled and its timber perhaps used to build the fire on which the victim was sacrificed. As late as 1538 an image carved from an oak was brought from Wales to London and there burned at Smithfield, together with a priest who bore the same name. Some giant oaks, however, retained their status as holy trees for generation after generation.

Onion – Onions were used as an instrument of divination by girls wishing to know the identity of their future husbands. On Christmas Eve a girl would take a number of onions and mark each with a label or a coded pattern of pins indicating the name of a man she fancied. The onions would then be hung in the chimney and the one which sprouted first would indicate her bridegroom.

Many cottage housewives used to keep an onion under the kitchen sink to attract germs – some still do. It was also thought that snakes had a strong aversion to the smell of onions. Onions were also widely used medicinally, especially to ward off a cold.

Orpine – A fleshy-leaved plant with a rosette of pink flowers, much used in divination. If a sprig of orpine is picked and hung upside down it will try to lift its head towards the light. On Midsummer Eve lovesick girls would use this propensity by hanging two sprigs side by side but a little distance apart, one dedicated to the girl and the other to her lover. If in the morning the two had bent towards each other the course of their love would run smoothly; but if away from each other, the romance was doomed.

Parsley – The correct day for sowing parsley is Good

Friday, on a rising moon. You must sow four times the amount of seed you need, to give the devil his quota. And the seed has to go down to hell and back nine times before it starts to germinate. Parsley should be sown at night and by the wife, rather than by her husband. But that is risky, for immediately she becomes pregnant.

Parsley should never be transplanted or given away or cut by a person in love. It is said to have been used by witches to procure abortions and that 'only the wicked can grow it'. When sown in rows, the rows must always run due north-south.

Peony – The superstitions about peony are all concerned with witchcraft. The dried roots, hung around the neck, are a charm against nightmares. They are also helpful to children teething. Peonies in the garden are also reputed to protect the house against evil spirits. But the roots have to be dug up by a dog, as it is dangerous for a human to do so.

Periwinkle – Once called the sorcerer's violet, it was used to garland medieval criminals on their way to the gallows. If worn as a button-hole by an unfaithful wife or a flirtatious girl it will speedily wither and die.

Rosemary – Supposed to be highly effective against witches. It should be dried and then used on May Day as a kind of exorcism to rid a house of witches or evil spirits. Rosemary can also be burnt, with rue, hemlock and blackthorn, to smoke out witches, but the exercise must be carried out by a man recently blessed by a Christian priest. It is still widely believed to flourish only where the wife rules the household.

Primrose – A single primrose brought into the house in spring or a primrose blooming in winter is said to be extremely unlucky, or even to foretell a death.

Rowan, or Mountain Ash – Not common enough as far south as Wiltshire for much folklore to become attached to it. Some rowans have been deliberately planted near farms as a protection against witchcraft, and cattle are believed to be especially vulnerable to witches around May Day. Rowan twigs were tied to buckets to prevent milk from going sour. Rowan gave protection against witchcraft in general but against the Evil Eye in particular, though some accounts insisted that the berries had to be eaten.

Sage – Sage will prosper as long as the master of the house is in good health. If rue be planted with sage it will prevent toads from poisoning the sage.

St John's-wort – Blooming at midsummer, the golden flowers of St John's-wort were associated with the midsummer sun and the golden flames of midsummer bonfires. An old name for it was amber, but when the pagan feast of Midsummer became the feast of St John the Baptist the flower naturally became St John's-wort.

Bunches of the flower were hung over doors of houses on Midsummer Eve to ward off witches and evil spirits, and whoever looked at a midsummer bonfire through the flowers of St John's-wort would find that the flames would never hurt their eyes, no matter how brightly they burned. If on Midsummer Eve you stepped on the plant a fairy horse would appear and carry you wherever you wished, but at the first rays of the rising sun it would leave you, wherever you happened to be. So great was the demand for the flowers during the festival that it was believed to be able to move about, to avoid would-be gatherers. The plant was said to be a sure protection against tempests and thunderstorms and an antidote to snakebite.

Tansy – Some women ate a salad of tansy leaves to procure a miscarriage; others to encourage conception. It lasts a long time and hence was laid on a corpse to preserve it until distant relatives had time to gather.

Sow-thistle – Mixed with toad spit this was used by witches for drawing a crooked cross on their bodies, thus rendering themselves invisible.

Vervain – Oil of vervain (verbena) was used to attract eels. If it was poured into a stream it would accumulate over the spot where a drowned body lay, and the eels would reveal the body's presence.

Vervain was much used by the Druids in divination. It had to be plucked at the moment when Sirius was rising, when neither moon nor sun was shining, and must be gathered with the left hand. No metal must touch the plant, which therefore had to be dug with a stag's antler. It was considered so valuable that a honeycomb had to be left on the spot as payment to the Earth Mother. The temples of Roman gods were swept with brooms of vervain, from which arose the custom of sweeping house floors with brooms of vervain to banish evil spirits. Vervain gave protection against witchcraft and was said to be a 'cure-all', including the bites of rabid animals.

Violet – Autumn-blooming violets were said to warn of a death. Worn as a necklace they were held to avert drunkenness.

Willow – Sawn willow is very unlucky, and few old-timers would have it in their houses; if it were admitted it had to be shaped with an adze. It was frequently used for constructing gibbets. But the gift of a willow branch on the morning of May Day would certainly be attended by good fortune.

Wormwood – A concoction made from wormwood was said to keep away fleas; and as these insects were generally held to be a plague sent by witches, it was held that wormwood was an effective deterrent against witches.

Yarrow – A witch had only to hold a sprig of yarrow over her eyes to acquire second sight. On the other hand, it could give protection against witches. No witch could step over yarrow strewn on the doorstep, and her spells could be nullified by giving her a yarrow-stuffed cushion to sit on.

Yew – The ancient trees so often found in churchyards, so gloomy at night, were made more sinister because they were thought to shelter witches. Ghosts were also said to haunt yew groves. Yew branches used to be placed under the corpse in its coffin. In many instances the presence of yew trees around a church are evidence that the church is occupying a site sacred to some earlier religion which treated yews as sacred.

12   Legends, Customs and Superstitions

The Aldbourne Dabchick – The villages of Aldbourne and Ramsbury provide a typical example of traditional feuds between neighbouring villages. Aldbourne is a downland village, with a stream that flows only in winter, leaving only a pond at other seasons; Ramsbury is a riverside village; yet it is Aldbourne which has associations with an essentially aquatic bird, the dabchick.

Aldbourne residents were known to their neighbours as 'Aldbourne dabchicks', and the Ramsbury children liked nothing better than to surreptitiously tie a dead dabchick to the back of the Aldbourne carrier's cart and then to shout, 'Yah! Aldbourne dabchicks!' That was in Victorian times. Earlier, the Aldbourne inhabitants took the epithet more seriously, and there was an old tradition that a person had to be ducked in Aldbourne pond before he was entitled to call himself an Aldbourne dabchick. Aldbourne was noted for its bell foundry, and the earliest bells bear the engraving of a small, long-necked bird which is evidently supposed to be a dabchick.

The local explanation of the origin of the name is that one day, long ago, a dabchick appeared on Aldbourne pond. No one knew what the bird was, so they sent for the oldest inhabitant, an ancient invalid who had to be brought to the pond in a wheelbarrow. He commanded the attendant to wheel him around the pond three times, whereupon he pronounced that the bird was a dabchick.

The story has several interesting elements. The dabchick seems to have been the totem of a tribe which settled at Aldbourne, having previously lived in a locality where the dabchick was common. In the ducking ceremony there is the vestige of an initiation ritual, similar to baptism. And the wheeling of the old man round the pond is said to be the survival of a solar myth, associated with the passage of the sun around the heavens.

Fairies – That many fairy stories derive from distant memories of ancient races of men, dispossessed by later invaders of our country, now meets with general acceptance. Tribes who possessed only flint tools were either enslaved or driven from their homes by newcomers equipped with bronze weapons. They, in turn, were superseded by new waves of invaders who had mastered the technique of smelting iron. The survivors of the older races retreated to the lonelier, wilder parts of our islands, where they lived a precarious existence in caves and woods – shy, elusive, yet from time to time needing contact with their neighbours.

Certain features common to many fairy stories fit in well with this notion. Fairies are small; and an alternative and frequently-used name for them is 'the little people'. The Iberian tribes which inhabited Britain in far-off times are known to have been small in stature. These early peoples had swarthy complexions and black hair. A frequent theme in fairy folklore is their occasional addiction to kidnapping babies, especially those with fair hair and blue eyes. Sometimes they left their own babies in exchange, and these were ugly, wizened little creatures with big ears. Fairy people were often clad in rags, appropriately for their way of life, but they did not covet fine clothes. Indeed, one way of frightening off fairies who were disposed to be of service to humans was to offer them new clothes. They used flint implements, and Stone Age flints found in fields were commonly known as 'elf arrows'. But they would have nothing to do with iron, which, indeed, could serve as a protection against fairy magic. Fairies could make themselves invisible, a belief which probably arose from the adroitness with which the primitive people of the hills and forests disappeared when scared, a skill acquired through long years of persecution.

All this has little in common with the way in which fairies are commonly portrayed as fragile, ethereal beings with wings, an image which derives largely from the imagination of romantic Victorian artists. Real fairies are more closely akin to brownies, pixies, gnomes, elves, goblins and other undersized sprites. The endearing qualities of the timid Stone Age people are demonstrated by the preponderance of stories in which fairies, brownies and the rest are kindly folk, more disposed to helping men than to harming them.

Of course, more fantastic lore became attached to them. Fairies and their kind dwelt in caves. Often they had been reported as disappearing into holes in hills, which were consequently believed to be hollow. Fairyland tended to become synonymous with the underworld, a shadowy reality, which the Celts called Annwn. The Celtic gods of lake and stream, of trees and standing stones and prehistoric monuments hence became merged with fairies.

One otherworldly feature of fairyland is that time is different from ours. Sometimes it moves at such a speed that a long sequence of events occurs in what to us is a mere second; indeed, there is a belief that fairies move so fast that one can hope to see them only as a momentary flash of movement out of the corner of one's eye. At other times it moves incredibly slowly, as in the tales of a person who sleeps on a fairy hill or is taken to fairyland for a single night and who wakes up to find he has been absent for twenty or thirty years.

In the Middle Ages fairies became associated with witchcraft and magic. As supernatural beings they were held to have strange powers, which a knowledgeable wizard might employ to his advantage.

Hobgoblins were a numerous race of fairy people, widely distributed throughout England. Many names of fields, lanes and other local features contain the element 'hob'. Very similar, though lazier, were the dobbies, who seldom wandered far from the farm they made their home. But knops were different, being hobgoblins with horses' heads. They were reputed to be savage, unpredictable creatures and are probably perpetuated in the hobby-horses which feature in pageants. There would seem to be a connection between horse-demons such as these and the Celtic horse-goddess, Epona.

The Horseman's Word – Many years ago – it must be nearly sixty – I worked for a time with an old chap who once confided to me that he was an initiate of the Society of Horsemen. He knew the secrets of the Horseman's Word. Recently I came across an old notebook in which I recorded what he told me, and it occurs to me that he may well have been the last survivor of the dying brotherhood. I have never since met anyone who professed any direct knowledge of it.

He said that the uncanny power ascribed to a member of the secret society was that an initiated horseman had only to whisper the appropriate secret word into a horse's ear to render it completely docile. A word from the horseman was sufficient to keep a horse safe in the stable or to arrest its movement in the open; neither force nor cajoling would move the animal till the horseman gave another word to release it.

The recognized date for the initiation ceremony, which took place at night in a deserted barn, was Martinmas (11 November). It was attended by thirteen persons, which suggests a resemblance to witchcraft, thirteen being the number of witches in a coven. Each member had to bring with him a pot of jam, a loaf of bread and a bottle of whisky.

Standing outside the door, the novice for initiation had to identify himself by a special knock and by answering a series of ritual questions, which were put to him by the 'Minister' who stood guarded by two sentinels armed with flails. He was then blindfolded before being allowed to enter and was led in with a halter around his neck. He had to swear a solemn oath that he would never reveal by word or by writing the secrets of the society.

The initiation ceremony proper, which began at midnight, started with the novice being required to take off his trousers. The Horseman's Word was then whispered to him. He also had to recite backwards a certain passage from the Bible, which, in an emergency, would summon the devil to his aid. As a test he was asked to write down the Word, but when he attempted to do so he received a painful rap on the knuckles, as a reminder that he had just sworn an oath never to do so!

Presently, to the reek of burning sulphur and the accompaniment of alarming noises, the arrival of the devil himself was announced, and the still-blindfolded initiate was invited to shake hands with him. He usually found himself grasping a cold, wet hoof, and when the blindfold was removed he saw the devil as a somewhat terrifying horned figure in a mask.

For the rest of the night, between bouts of eating and drinking, the brethren imparted to their new recruit the secrets of the society. He learned, for instance, the horseman's handshake, which identified a fellow member; also a method of tying the plough-rein and many practical matters dealing with the management of horses.

Unfortunately here the old man's memory became a little confused, for on another occasion he spoke of a different initiation ritual. This involved catching a live toad and pegging it to an ant-heap until the ants had eaten the bones clean. Alternatively the toad could be thrown to the ground with sufficient force to kill it. The bones were then carried in the pocket until they were thoroughly dry.

Then, on the night of a full moon, the man had to go down to a stream and throw in the bones, which were said to scream horribly in the process. One bone would detach itself from the rest and start to move upstream. This one had to be retrieved by the Toadman, who then had to carry it to the stable on three consecutive nights. On the third night the devil would appear.

There was a standard demonstration of the Toadman's power over horses. An ordinary garden fork was stuck into a heap of straw and one or two powerful horses were hitched to it. Try as they would they could not shift it. But when the Toadman gave the word or sign one horse could move it easily.

While there can be no doubt that initiated horsemen possessed this power over horses we can only speculate how it worked. One theory is that certain aromatic substances were employed and were secretly rubbed on some part of the horse when the horseman stooped down, ostensibly to feel its fetlock. A mixture of oil of origanum, oil of rosemary, oil of cinnamon and oil of fennel was said to be effective in controlling an unruly animal, and this may have been the secret substance, or one of them, used by the Toadmen. It was given to the horse on lumps of sugar. While it could immobilize a horse an antidote could be supplied by a hand covered with milk and vinegar.

Old-time carters would keep a brown paper parcel of clipped yew leaves from a female tree under their bed for a year or more, before adding a little to a horse's rations to make its coat shine or generally improve its appearance. A mixture of garlic, liquorice and aniseed was said to work wonders but was specifically recommended for a horse suffering from nightmares! Chopped walnut leaves were said to be good for worming horses. Sores on horses could be cured by gathering red thistles before daybreak and putting one on each of the four quarters of a compass, with a stone in the middle. Marchwort in the drinking water of horses was reputed to be effective in keeping the animals healthy, but the herb must be picked with the left hand only, and without looking back!

Birth Lore – Childbirth was a time of such anxiety that all possible precautions had to be taken. Indeed, they had to be continued throughout the infancy of the child, for until recent years the chances of it surviving to its fifth birthday were no more than even, while the death of either mother or child during the birth was common.

During the final stages of pregnancy the mother-to-be kept herself out of sight as far as possible, lest she attract the attention of evil influences. There was also the matter of birthmarks, which were held to result from a mother being frightened by some animal or spirit during pregnancy.

Fairies were also on the look-out for pregnant mothers so that at the critical moment they could snatch the baby and substitute one of their own. Because changeling children were thought never to do well, unhealthy children were considered to be changelings or fairy children. To avoid such a disaster, incessant watch had to be kept over the child for the first few days and nights of its life. Female relatives took turns in watching the cradle. To ward off possible dangers of this sort special cakes were made and pieces were distributed to anyone encountered, especially strangers. One never knew who might be a fairy or a witch in disguise. Black cocks could, however, penetrate the disguise and crow to warn of the danger. This power was not possessed by white cocks. Fire-irons placed over the cradle in the shape of a cross were a reasonably effective protection, as were salt, iron and the Bible.

The special cake made for general distribution was not the same as the 'groaning cake', which was prepared for the mother to eat when she felt the first pains. As the recipe for that cake included a quantity of powdered hemp seed the obvious purpose was to ease the labour pains. When the birth was over, the mother was given a concoction in which rum butter was the chief ingredient, as a tonic.

Midwives were often credited with second sight as they frequently managed to arrive as soon as the birth had started, even though they had not been summoned. The notion that at childbirth the father suffered pains similar to those of the mother was widespread. In some districts the father was put to bed. The belief was sometimes put to practical use in the case of an unmarried mother; the neighbours looked around for a man in bed with stomach pains!

Certain dates and times were lucky or unlucky for a birth; the first day of May was considered so unlucky that, if all measures to promote the birth on 30 April failed, the midwife would give the mother a draught to send her to sleep for twenty-four hours. On the other hand, a child born between Friday midnight and Saturday dawn would be exceptionally lucky. In particular, it would possess certain magical qualities, such as the gift of second sight, an immunity from witchcraft, power over animals, and skill in medicines.

In times past the caul, or part of the placental membrane which covers the child's head at birth, was carefully preserved as a talisman. It not only brought good luck but was a protection for travellers, especially by sea. It also gave its owner the gift of oratory.

If the end of a very bright rainbow appeared to rest on a house, a boy baby would be born there within the next year. If a boy baby were born during a waning moon, the next child would be a girl and vice versa; but a baby born during a waxing moon would ensure that the next baby would be of the same sex. Everyone who came to visit a newborn baby or its parents should bring a present. A child should not be named after a relative recently or prematurely dead, or its spirit might, by confusion of identity, be prematurely summoned to the afterworld.

As soon as possible after the birth a child should be

baptized and its mother churched. Both ceremonies were held to give magical protection. But it was important for the child to be carried upstairs before being taken downstairs, for this would ensure that he would 'rise in life'. Should a woman want no more children she should keep the cradle in the house and on no account give it away, or another birth would assuredly follow. For the first year of its life a child should not be weighed, should not have its finger-nails cut (they should be bitten off by its mother) and should not have its hands washed (or its luck would be washed away).

Conception could be aided by eating tansy or drinking tea made from an infusion of mandrake but could be prevented by sleeping with corpse money under the pillow. Corpse money was a coin that had been held in the hand of a dead person for two minutes or more. A miscarriage could be brought on by eating horseradish leaves or hemp leaves (cannabis), though the horseradish had to be eaten three times a day for three days.

For a baby to cry during the baptismal ceremony is thought to be a good omen.

Finger-nails – Most people know the formula for telling one's fortunes from the white spots on the nails of the right hand (though some say it should be the left hand). Starting with the thumb the incantation runs: 'A gift; a friend; a foe; a lover; a journey to go.' Yellow spots on the nails are a sign of approaching death; blue specks, of misfortune.

To cut one's nails on a Friday or a Sunday is unlucky. However, that taboo restricts one's choice less than the rule in ancient Rome, which was that nails should be cut only on the ninth day of the month. The person who, in a married couple, can cut the nails of his or her right hand with scissors held in the left will be master of the house. To avoid danger, the thumb should be doubled back into the palm so that the nail is concealed.

The Hand of Glory – Tradition has it that the hand of a

dead murderer has special magical powers. In particular, it can act as a narcotic, useful to thieves in keeping a household asleep while they were busy. One recipe is that the hand has to be dried in the smoke of juniper and yew. Then a candle has to be fashioned from the fat of a bear, a badger and an unbaptized child. Placed in the Hand of Glory this would ensure, with the proper incantations and ritual, that the victims would stay asleep as long as the candle burned.

A somewhat similar superstition was that a cure for cancer was to rub the affected part of the body with a dead woman's hand. Examples are known of sufferers asking to be allowed to rub themselves with the hand of a woman recently dead but not yet buried.

Holed Flints – Holed flints have long been regarded as effective protection against witchcraft. They may still be seen hanging over the doors of cottages and stables. They would in particular prevent witches from 'borrowing' horses and riding them all night and would also ward off witch-borne diseases. They can be used in the treatment of certain human ailments, notably cramp, for which one keeps a holed flint under the bed.

Moon Lore – Superstitions concerning the moon are numerous. It is unlucky to see the new moon through glass. When you see the new moon for the first time, turn your money. An old tradition says that you should bow, turn around three times (or nine times) and curtsy. Seeds must always be sown when the moon is waxing, except for beans and peas which are best sown during a waning moon. Hair must be cut and pigs killed only during a waxing moon, but trees should be felled as the moon wanes.

For the moon to shine on one's face is not only unlucky but dangerous. My mother, in the 1890s, always carried a parasol when walking in the woods by moonlight. Fairies and witches were particularly active on moonlit nights, and the association of the moon with mental aberrations (lunacy) is extremely ancient (and seems to have some basis in fact).

> All hail to thee, Moon! All hail to thee!
> I pray thee, good Moon, declare to me
> This night who my husband shall be,

was an incantation recited to the first new moon of the new year by maidens seeking to peer into the future. According to some versions, the girl has to stand with her feet on a stone firmly embedded in the earth and with her back to a tree for the charm to be fully effective.

Some of the circles of standing stones in Britain are associated with moon lore, especially those which are said to be dancers turned to stone.

The Lore of Odd Numbers – For some reason odd numbers seem always to have been the subject of superstitious regard. The best-known example today is the number thirteen, which, of course, is considered extremely unlucky. The belief is said to be based on the fact that thirteen persons were present at the Last Supper, but witch covens consisting of thirteen members are probably older than that explanation.

Seven is regarded as a particularly lucky number, perhaps because of the frequency with which it is mentioned in the Bible. Three and nine are similarly favoured numbers. In many ancient ceremonies, including some which survive as children's games, the company has to dance around an object, often a sacred stone, three times, or sometimes three times three – nine.

A combination of odd numbers also has great significance. Seven times nine are sixty-three, for which reason the sixty-third year of a man's life is particularly hazardous. If he manages to survive it he is likely to live to a good old age. The seventh son of a seventh son is supposed to be endowed with remarkable gifts, including that of second sight. Druids embarking on a programme of cursing an unsatisfactory king would institute a fast, involving seven of them. At sunrise they would assemble at a spot where seven farms met, stand with each one of the seven on a different farm, and there engage in a fairly elaborate ritual with many incantations.

Second Sight – Throughout the ancient world oracles which uttered cryptic prophecies were held in high regard. In Britain soothsaying Druids would slaughter a sacrificial bull, eat a heavy meal of its flesh and then wrap themselves for sleep in the hide. The hypnotic trance in which they then predicted the future was known as the 'bull-dream'.

The custom of 'scrying' or crystal-gazing was widespread. The technique consists of staring fixedly at a bright surface while repeating a formula over and over again and can produce, especially in a susceptible person, a kind of hypnotic state in which kaleidoscopic visions may be seen. The traditional object is a crystal ball, but any brilliant surface will do.

Utterances made by those who claimed to look into the future seem to have been essentially visual. Sufficient evidence exists to lead us to believe that some visions may have been induced by hallucinatory drugs. References to hemp seed (cannabis) and opiates in old-time folklore are common.

Wedding Lore – Superstitions and beliefs relating to weddings are innumerable, ranging from divination to discover one's true love to the minutest details of dress and behaviour at the wedding ceremony. There are so many taboos that one wonders how anyone ever managed to get married at all.

For instance, it was unlucky to get married in Lent. It was unlucky to get married in May. It was unlucky to get married between haymaking and harvest. It was unlucky to get married on a Friday. It was unlucky to get married during a thunderstorm. It was unlucky to get married when the moon was waning, or when the tide was ebbing.

A medieval church guide to dates for marriages excludes December, the period from late January to Easter, and the first three weeks of May. The best day of a week for a wedding was Thursday, with Tuesday the next best.

However, there was an obvious conflict between the recommendations of the Church and the traditions of older religions, and in practice the latter usually won. Medieval records of weddings during Lent and even on Good Friday are quite frequent. The older tradition maintained that March and September were the best months for weddings. The luckiest pair of all were those on whose wedding-bed the harvest moon shone.

Apart from the church calendar, the old customs seem to be largely dictated by practical considerations. The prejudice against summer weddings reflects the conviction that in an agricultural community everybody is too busy in the summer months. The ill-luck attached to May weddings may well be attributed to action by priests of the Christian church who were often scandalized by what went on in the woods on the eve of May Day. An alternative suggestion is that in Roman times May was associated with Lemuralia, the festival of the dead. Anything to do with death was to be avoided, and to meet a funeral procession on the way to church to be married was considered most unlucky.

Certain days were propitious for peering into the future. If on St Agnes's Eve (20 January) a girl was looking over a gate when she first saw the new moon and then went home and said her prayers she would dream of her future lover. Or she could make a Dumb Cake, which she had to prepare and put to bake without uttering a word At midnight the ghost of her future husband would come and turn the cake for her. Sometimes she had the help of other girls, which made the rule of silence more difficult. And sometimes the cake had special ingredients, including, besides the normal ones, salt, eggshells and even soot. She had to eat a slice of it before retiring to bed, walking backwards! Alternatively, she had to eat part of a stolen salt herring, and during the night her future husband would bring her a glass of water.

A common form of divination was to peel an apple in one continuous strip and toss the peel over her left shoulder. Falling to the floor, it was supposed to form the initial of her future husband's name. As an alternative a girl could confine snails in a box overnight, and in the morning the slimy trails would form the young man's initial.

Many former Christmas traditions were transferred to St Thomas's Day (21 December). On that date a girl could dream of her true love by peeling a large onion just before going to bed, sticking nine pins into it and repeating a magic formula. Or she could go out to the henhouse and peep in at midnight. If the cock crowed before the hens cackled she would be married within a year.

In summer the yarrow flowers offered a potent medium for divination. A girl needed to pick a bunch of them while walking barefoot in a meadow at midnight under a full moon. She had to place them under her bed and if, in the morning, they were still wet with dew she might soon expect a proposal of marriage.

A sure way to dream of the husband-to-be was for the girl to place her shoes in the form of a T by her bed on Hallowe'en. The letter T represented the hammer of the Norse god Thor and was a very powerful charm. Pinning her garters to the wall on the same night helped matters. And of course a custom with the same purpose, still widely observed, is to sleep with a slice of wedding-cake under the pillow.

There are a mass of wedding taboos. Most brides avoid wearing green, but few know that is because green was supposed to be a fairy colour and to wear it might put the bride into the power of the fairies. White, the colour of virginity, is the favourite; gold and silver are the next best; but yellow and purple should be avoided. It is unlucky for a bride to make her own wedding-dress or to try on the complete outfit before the wedding morning. The veil should always be left until last, put on just before she leaves the house. That is the only occasion on which she should see herself in a mirror while wearing her veil. It is better not to complete the sewing of the wedding-dress until the wedding morning. And, of course, the bridegroom must not see her on the wedding-day before she enters the church. The old maxim, that the bride should wear 'something old, something new, something borrowed and something blue', is still widely honoured.

The belief that it is lucky to see a sweep on leaving the church after a wedding is still well known. In some districts it is customary for him to kiss the bride at the church door. A logical explanation sometimes advanced is that the contrast between her own pristine whiteness and the sweep's grimy face and clothes would be so dramatic that she would ever afterwards have a horror of dirt and become a tidy housewife. The truth is that in ancient times soot was associated with fertility. Until quite recent times the old custom of strewing the church path with flowers and grains of wheat as the couple left the church was still maintained. This, too, was originally a fertility rite, as was the custom of throwing rice, latterly confetti, over the bride and groom.

Sometimes the way from the church is obstructed by a barrier, and the bridegroom has to pay a toll to have it removed. And sometimes the church gates are tied, in which case the knots have to be patiently undone by the bridegroom, who must on no account cut any of them. This closely resembles the tradition that on the wedding-night the bridegroom has to undress the bride, carefully untying every knot fastening her gown. Failure to do so will result in her having difficulty in conceiving. Barring the church gate does not, however, apply to lychgates; bridal parties must never, unless there is no other way, pass through one of them, because of their association with funerals.

In old times only the gentry went to and left the church in

carriages; ordinary folk had 'walking weddings'. After leaving the church the wedding party would line up and, headed by the bride and groom, walk to the home of the bride's parents, calling at the cottages of friends and relations on the way.

Arriving at their new home after the ceremony, the bridegroom has to carry the bride over the threshold. The custom is associated with the tradition that the bride must never be addressed by her married name before the wedding or by her single name afterwards. The common object of these traditions is to deceive any evil spirits or bearers of ill-luck that may be lurking with evil intent. By completely severing the links with her former life and even her former identity she is enabled to start afresh, unhampered by any past misfortunes. One of the chief props of a marriage was a besom, to sweep away all traces of unhappy links with the past.

Nowadays the bride and groom usually join hands to cut the wedding-cake, but in times past this was the sole duty of the bride. Concealed in the cake were a ring and a thimble. The girl who acquired the ring would be the next to wed, but the one who had the thimble felt sure she was doomed to be an old maid.

Death Lore – Death portents are many and varied. They include a clock stopping or striking thirteen; a robin entering a house; an owl hooting or a dog howling near a house where a sick person is lying; a cock crowing at night; mice or crickets leaving a house; the presence of a corpse in a house over Sunday; a mirror falling and shattering; a frog entering a house; an umbrella open indoors; the sound of the death-watch beetle; the first cuckoo of the year if heard while lying in bed; and so on, almost *ad infinitum*.

When candles were in common use the melting wax would sometimes curl over into what was held to be the shape of a coffin handle – a very bad omen. On certain nights, notably St Mark's Eve or St Agnes's Eve, a person watching a church doorway might see passing through it in procession the ghosts of those parishioners who would die in the coming year. It is on record that a certain sexton was in the habit of doing so in order to calculate his likely income in the next year from grave-digging!

When death seemed inevitable, relatives considered it their duty to make the passing as easy as possible. An old custom, which must have precluded all chance of recovery, was to take the dying person out of bed and lay him on the earthen floor. 'Earth to earth ...' Or the pillow would be drawn away suddenly. On the other hand, death might be delayed, though not averted, by supporting the patient on feather pillows, especially those stuffed with the feathers of birds, as distinct from those of domestic poultry. Death could also be eased by orientating the bed the same way as the floorboards.

At the moment of death, doors and windows should be opened and all domestic animals turned out, lest the departing spirit enter one of them. Likewise mirrors should be covered and the fire extinguished. As soon as possible after the death, the passing bell should be tolled.

The assumption was that the tolling informed the neighbours of the death, but in earlier times it had two other purposes. One was to provide the departing soul with a suitable send-off, and the prayers of all good Christians accompanied the sound of the bell. The other was as a protection against evil spirits 'who stood ready about the Bed's foot and about the House, ready to seize their prey or at least to molest and terrify the Soul in its passage; but by the ringing of that Bell (for Evil Spirits are much afraid of Bells) they were kept aloof; and the Soul, like a hunted Hare, gained the start'. Because of this awesome threat to the departing soul, it seems that the former custom was to toll the bell *before* the death.

While in the house the corpse must never be left alone, or in the dark; hence the custom of keeping a vigil or wake. A wake in Wiltshire was a somewhat solemn and sad affair, though there is evidence that it was once much livelier – a fine send-off party for the deceased. In some places the custom of touching the corpse may be still observed. This may be a form of respect, but in the case of violent death it was said that the touch of the murderer's hand would cause the corpse to bleed.

Salt used to be placed on the breast of the corpse, this being a powerful protection against demons. Sometimes a candle was also added. The ancient custom of putting a coin in the mouth of the deceased, to pay the bill of the ferryman to the underworld, was, surprisingly, still observed in some places in the nineteenth century.

An old custom, now probably obsolete, was for a person or persons to eat a ritual meal, including some of the salt that had been on the deceased's breast. This was known as sin-eating, for by it the sins of the dead person were transferred to the partakers. Often professional sin-eaters were hired for the purpose.

On the day of the funeral the corpse had to be taken out of the house feet first. Rosemary and evergreens were placed with it in the coffin. The bearers led the funeral procession to the lychgate, where the clergyman took over, and it was unlucky for anyone to pass in front of it on the journey. Sometimes the mourners insisted on observing the old custom of carrying the coffin three times sunwise around the church. Rain on the coffin was considered a good thing for the deceased; it would help his journey to Paradise.

It used to be held, without legal foundation, that to admit the passage of a corpse along any road or path was to establish a right of way. Many disputes have arisen from this belief.

13 Ghosts Miscellaneous

THE WHITE BIRDS OF SALISBURY PLAIN

The legend of the white birds of Salisbury Plain, which are said to accompany the death of a bishop of Salisbury, has its origin no further back than 1885. They were seen at that time rising from the ground in the palace gardens and sailing away westwards just before the death of Bishop Moberly. They were seen by Miss Moberly, who described them as large birds, like albatrosses, with dazzling white wings which they did not flap as they flew.

Miss Edith Olivier next saw them in 1911. She had taken the Wilton choirboys on their annual outing and was returning with them in a wagonette towards evening. She noticed two white birds, which seemed to be floating through the air rather than flying, over meadows at Hurdcott. On reaching home she was greeted with the news that Bishop Wordsworth, Bishop of Salisbury, had died unexpectedly that day, while his family were attending a flower show. She did not know of the legend at the time, but when she heard it, she put two and two together.

Those are the only two references to the legend that I have been able to discover, and they illustrate how slender is the evidence on which such legends can arise. It is as well to remember that before the twentieth century the presence of gulls inland was by no means the everyday event it has since become. Neither Miss Moberly nor Miss Olivier would have been sufficiently familiar with a gull to identify it at a glance. The flight, described as floating through the air, is typical of that of a gull that has recently taken wing and is surveying its surroundings. The apparent size of the birds can be discounted. We are left with the coincidence of the appearance of the birds with the deaths of two bishops of Salisbury. Well, we must make what we choose of that, but my preference is that the birds were gulls.

There are two other Wiltshire stories of the uncanny appearance of birds. The Revd W. Fowler, a canon of Lincoln, retired to a rectory in Wiltshire to write a book on birds. On the day of his death all the owls in the neighbourhood seemed to have gathered around his house, perching on the roof, gateposts and pinnacles. There they remained until he was dead, when they all disappeared. Then, on the day of the funeral, when the coffin was being carried under the lychgate to the church, a large white owl swooped down, almost touching the coffin, before retiring to a large yew tree in the churchyard. This strikes me as being more credible than the bishops' white birds, though it would be good to have further details.

A large white bird is said to rise from the ground at midnight near the top of Clyffe Hall Hill, Market Lavington. It was seen by a lady who was born in 1827, who described it as a huge bird that suddenly rose up from the ground on a dark night, causing her horse to shy.

There is also the story of Bishop Hallom, of Salisbury, who died in 1414 while attending the Council of Constance, in Switzerland. During his lying-in-state a great flock of birds alighted on the roof of the hall and stayed there all night, uttering harsh, discordant cries. Obviously migrants; they had all gone by the morning.

THE PACT

This is a story related by Peter Underwood, president of The Ghost Club. It concerns three young officers who, many years ago, enjoyed a comradeship that went on for years. At last, however, the time came for it to be broken.

'We celebrated the end by a terrific binge at a final guest night – walking back to our quarters, arm in arm, as signs of dawn were in the sky ... And we three then and there made a pact that whoever died first would come back for the next to go and whoever died last would be welcomed by the other two.'

The narrator went on, 'A year later one died in India of malaria, and soon after the other was killed in a rail accident. I remained. And years passed.'

In his retirement the colonel, as he had by then become, was confronted by an upsetting experience. A subaltern had reported a ghost seen in the mess ante-room. It was standing in front of the fireplace, dressed in an old-fashioned high-collared mess jacket and appeared so natural that the subaltern, taking him for a guest, offered him a drink. The figure looked at him steadfastly ... and then vanished.

The colonel gave orders that the occurrence was not to be discussed and so the memory began to fade. Then, one evening, when he was sitting in the mess alone, looking through the illustrated weeklies, he glanced up and saw an officer in the old mess kit standing a couple of paces away and looking at him. Their eyes met, and he smiled. It was his old friend. Then he vanished.

The incident so troubled the colonel that he sent for a couple of colleagues whom he knew were interested in the occult, and they came down to visit him at his quarters at Bulford, on Salisbury Plain. After entertaining them to a meal he got out an album of old photographs and, calling in the young subaltern, asked whether he could identify any one of the subjects.

Presently the young man pointed to a photo and said, 'That is the man I saw.' It was the friend who had died of malaria those many years ago. The subaltern identified the same man in two other photographs.

The colonel entertained his guests to dinner in the mess room.

The dinner passed, as mess dinners do, to be succeeded by talk, decorous and staid, which, according to unwritten law, gradually ceased to be either decorous or staid. The noise of good fellowship increased to pandemonium, to shouts and songs and to taunts and sham physical violence.

Stuart came up to me and said, 'I'm off. The Mess is hotting up, when it's best for commanding officers to be neither seen nor heard. Are you coming or would you like to stay on?'

We consulted and then replied, 'No, we must stay on to the end.'

Stuart replied with a laugh, 'As you wish, but don't blame me if old bones get the worst of battles with young ones.'

… An hilarious hour passed and waned. Guests and older members departed, and just a few remained. Suddenly Douglas asked the young subaltern and myself to have a quiet word with him and he led us across the room to sit isolated on the padded guard rail of the fireplace. The mess ante-room was more or less empty and somewhat disconsolate to look at.

The three of us sat in a row, Douglas in the middle, and after a moment he said, 'Look across the room. Do you see anything?'

The subaltern turned his head and started visibly, and would have stood up in his excitement if Douglas's restraining hand had not held his still.

'I see three men,' he said. 'Three subalterns in the old mess kit. They are standing in front of the other fireplace and looking at the chaps round the piano. The one on the right is the man I saw here before. The one on the left I don't know. Now they have linked arms with the middle figure and they are smiling at each other and seem very happy.'

He stopped speaking for a moment and then went on, 'It's strange, but if he were not so young and not in that old-fashioned kit, I'd swear the middle fellow was our Colonel.'

'You would not have been wrong,' said Douglas.

'What do you mean?' the subaltern asked, then, looking across the room, he added, 'Oh, they're fading away.'

'They're gone,' Douglas whispered, but I had seen nothing anyway.

Some minutes later a resounding knock sounded on the door and in walked the NCO of the quarter Guard and a policeman.

… A whisper licked around the room like a fire along a powder train.

'What?'

'Yes, the Colonel. Killed by a lorry.'

The three wise men were together again.

THE DRUMMER OF SALISBURY PLAIN

Gervase Matcham and John Sheppard were two sailors paid off after a spell of duty on board a man-of-war and making their way inland, glad to be on dry land again. It was June 1786. They were approaching Salisbury when they were overtaken by a sudden thunderstorm, which seemed to burst on them with considerable violence.

Matcham was scared out of his wits and began to blurt out a confession. He dashed hither and thither, fell to the ground begging for mercy and pleaded with Sheppard that, if they survived the storm, he would see that they should be taken before magistrates in the first town they came to. The storm passed and the next morning the two men appeared before the mayor of Salisbury, to whom Matcham recounted the following story.

Seven years earlier he was walking along a country road between Alconbury and Bugden, in Huntingdonshire, with a 17-year-old drummer boy named Jones, whose father was a recruiting sergeant. They walked together, chatting quite amicably, until they passed an inn and

Matcham suggested that they drop in for a drink. The boy refused, whereupon Matcham lost his temper and struck a blow which felled him to the ground. As he stood over him he suddenly thought of the money the boy was carrying and of how easy it would be to relieve him of it. He stooped down to do so, but the boy recovered his senses and began to fight back. In a flash, Matcham drew out a knife and slit the boy's throat.

Matcham duly repeated his story to the magistrate but, having by now recovered from his fright during the thunderstorm, refused to sign it. The mayor thought at first that his mind was deranged but decided that he ought to make some enquiries so committed him to custody until he had been in touch with Huntingdon.

In due course the Huntingdon coroner wrote to the mayor confirming the story. He did not recognize the name Matcham but remembered that the man who had been sought in connection with the murder had a front tooth missing. The Salisbury mayor had Matcham's mouth examined and found indeed that a front tooth was missing. And Matcham confessed that he had enlisted under the name of Jarvis, as he had recently deserted from another ship.

So Matcham was duly hanged, through the prickings of a guilty conscience aroused by a thunderstorm.

RUTH PIERCE OF DEVIZES

In Devizes market-place there stands a memorial that records 'an awful event which occurred in this market place in the year 1753, a salutary warning of improperly invoking divine vengeance or of calling on the holy name of God to conceal the devices of falsehood and fraud'.

On 25 January 1753, Ruth Pierce and three other women agreed to buy a sack of wheat. All undertook to pay equal shares, but when the money was counted it was found to be short. One of the other women accused Ruth Pierce of withholding her share and demanded that she pay up.

Whereupon Ruth declared that she had already paid her share and wished that she might drop dead if she had not done so. A crowd gathered at the sound of the quarrel, and Ruth Pierce emphatically repeated her wish. Whereupon she dropped dead, and the missing money was found grasped in her hand.

MURDER AT MARKET LAVINGTON

The White Lady of Market Lavington haunts one of the rooms of the old parsonage and has been seen by many people. She appears suddenly and passes through doors and walls as though they didn't exist. People who have slept in the room which she particularly frequents have found themselves awakened by someone pinching their toes or slapping their face. No one has ever seen the face of the White Lady because of her hood, which always hides the face in deep shadow.

One popular explanation of the haunting is that the lady severed an artery in the body of her stepson and watched him bleed to death. She pretended that he had been playing with a knife and had accidentally cut himself. Not long afterwards she was thrown from her horse while hunting and seriously injured. When she realized that she had not long to live she confessed to the crime. But why she committed it is not explained.

OLIVE'S LEAP

In the reign of Queen Elizabeth I the manor of Lacock was inherited by Sir Henry Sharington, who had exaggerated ideas of his own importance and who strenuously objected to his youngest daughter's choice of lover. In fact, he forbade her to meet him or have any contact with him.

One evening as she was walking on the battlements of her home she suddenly saw her lover creeping stealthily through the gardens. He was hoping to see her and engage a few words from her, even if only from a distance.

Impulsively, she decided that the enforced separation had gone on long enough and took a flying leap into the garden far below. The young man saw her coming and stood rooted to the spot. The wind caught in her swirling skirts and let her down lightly but, unfortunately, right on top of the young man, who was knocked out. Olive was aghast and ran quickly for help, forgetting about the need for secrecy.

However, all ended well. Sir Henry was so shaken by his daughter's resolution that he withdrew his objections and agreed to the wedding. 'Since she made such a leap, she should e'en marry him,' was his resigned summing-up of the situation.

HIDDEN TREASURE

I am indebted to Peter Underwood, in his book *Ghosts of Wiltshire*, for the following story.

Lord Castletown, as a young boy, was taken to spend Christmas at the home of family friends near Bradford-on-Avon. Nearby was an old manor, built around 1640 and reputed to be haunted but at the time uninhabited, with only a caretaker in charge. On Christmas Eve conversation drifted to the haunted house and a party of young people decided to spend the night there. After a merry evening they made their way to the house, tired and contented, and were soon fast asleep.

During the night Lord Castletown woke with a start and was surprised to see the face of an unknown person looking down at him. He was not frightened, for it was a kind face, and it occurred to him that it might be the caretaker, whom he had not met. And then he noticed that the apparition had no lower limbs!

She beckoned to him and he found himself getting out of bed, preparing to follow her. He noticed that she was wearing a long white dress that swayed from side to side. She led him out of the bedroom, along a corridor and through a succession of passages. He seemed to be walking in a dream and didn't feel the cold. Eventually they arrived in one of the oldest parts of the house, at a room which he had not even known existed. His guide circled the room and then rested at a corner, pointing to a spot in the wall. She became quite still – and vanished!

He managed, with difficulty for he had no light, to find his way back to his room, and soon fell fast asleep. In the morning he at first thought it must have been a dream but noticed that his feet were black with dust and dirt. So he confided in his uncle, who accompanied him to the room in question and carefully marked the spot indicated by the ghost. 'Immediately after Christmas a mason was called in, and the wall in the room was broken down at the spot indicated by the ghost and there, in a sort of recess, were found a lot of family jewels and plate that had been lost for many years.'

CANINE EVIDENCE

A farmer who lived at Little Cuckoo Farm, Urchfont, went to market one day and conducted some successful transactions. He returned home and went to bed early, being an old man. A man who had witnessed his bargains called at his house, murdered the old man and stole the gold. Then, shutting the dog in the house, he went off to Tilshead and proceeded to get drunk on the money. By chance, a neighbour called at the farm and, getting no reply, went inside and found the corpse of the murdered farmer. He let the dog out, and the animal sniffed around for a bit and then made off for Tilshead, where he led the searchers to the murderer, who was very much the worse for drink. He was later hanged from a gallows erected in a field on the farm.

A RASCALLY INNKEEPER

The Shepherd and Dog was the name of a little thatched inn, long since disappeared, at a place called Lydeway, in a lonely spot of the Andover to Devizes road. Rumours circulated that certain wealthy-looking travellers who spent the night there were never heard of again. The landlord was a rascal named Thomas Burry.

One night a customer named Mr Withers overheard a conversation of a plot to murder a Scottish pedlar who was staying the night at the inn. He straightway left the inn and ran all the way to Urchfont, where he told his neighbours what was afoot. A party of them went with him back to the inn and rescued the pedlar through a bedroom window.

Enquiries were made and a trap-door was discovered in a private room where Thomas Burry used to invite his guests for a drink. While the guest was drinking a bolt was drawn, precipitating the victim into a cellar, where he was robbed and murdered. The body was then buried in a field behind the inn, and more than a dozen corpses were disinterred from shallow graves. Many years after Burry's death another skeleton with his head bashed in was also found.

Records are silent as to what happened to Burry, though doubtless he was hanged. It is remembered, however, that the bells of Stert church, where the funeral was held, refused to sound when Burry was buried.

A LONGLEAT TRAGEDY

The wife of the second Viscount Weymouth of Longleat was a strikingly beautiful woman, who attracted a lover. Discovering this, the Viscount fought a duel with him in a passage at the top of the house and killed him. Many years later, in the time of the fifth Marquess (who died in 1946) a body was discovered buried in the cellars. He was wearing jackboots, which crumbled away when exposed to air.

The passage where the duel was fought is now known as 'The Green Lady's Walk' and is said to be haunted by the ghost of Lady Louisa Carteret, the lady in question.

SKIMMETING AND HOOSIT-HUNTING

'Skimmeting', also called 'rough music', was a communal attempt to shame a wife-beater or, occasionally, an adulterer. My father could just remember a skimmeting which took place at Pitton when he was a small boy, in the early 1880s. A large party of villagers, armed with tin trays, drums and anything else that made a noise, assembled outside the man's house. There for about an hour they jeered, shouted abuse at him and made as much racket as possible. They came well provided with lumps of cowdung, rotten eggs, buckets full of slops and other unpleasant objects, which they hoped to throw at him if he showed his face, but he did not, so they contented themselves with throwing their missiles at the door and windows. My father could not remember what offence the man had committed but thought it had been a flagrant affair with another man's wife.

Earlier accounts of the custom make a distinction between skimmeting, which was applied to wife-beaters and apparently at times to hen-pecked husbands, and the 'Hoosit Hunt', a penalty for immorality. Details of the two, and the difference between them, were recorded and summarized in an article 'Moonrake Medley', which appeared in the *Wiltshire Archaeological Magazine*, vol 50 (1943). It reads:

A paper by F.A. Carrington, of Ogbourne St George, on certain ancient Wiltshire customs appeared in our very first number, just ninety years ago, and one of the customs described is the 'Wooset'. (The 'W' is silent.) Carrington had seen two – one at Burbage in 1835, the other at Ogbourne St George about 1840. From his description they seemed to lack little or nothing of their earlier elaboration, the processions taking place on nine nights out of a consecutive fifteen. Both, it should be noted, dealt with cases of conjugal infidelity. Skimmeting was reserved for hen-pecked husbands.

The two processions, he says, were different. The rough band of frying-pans, old kettles filled with stones, sheep's horns, cracked sheep-bells, discarded fish-kettle beaten with a marrow-bone, or any other instrument, we may suppose, supplied by the village dump, doubtless figured in both. However, in place of the seven-foot cross carrying a chemise on its arms and on its head a horse's skull with a pair of deer's horns attached, which formed the main exhibit of the 'Ooset', the principal group in the skimmeting was the stuffed figure of a man placed on horseback, with a man in woman's clothes riding behind him, beating the figure about the head with a wooden ladle ...

A personal account of an Oosit Hunt, by a Mr E.R. Pole, is then given:

Mr Richard Hill of Ramsbury remembers clearly that when a lad of about ten years old he saw 'Oosit Hunting' at Ramsbury in the year 1868 or 1869. A man known to have been unfaithful to his wife, although they had a large family (for that reason the name is withheld) was the object.

A procession was formed led by a man holding the skeleton of a horse's head on a stick, its jaws made to open and shut by pulling a string, with a rough band consisting of trumpets, trombones, kettle-drums, etc., followed by a rabble with pots and pans and anything they could make a noise on or with. They paraded up to and around the man's house for three or four nights, each night the crowd increasing. The police tried to stop them but were unable to do so.

Smock weddings belong to an earlier age but are worth a mention. It used to be generally believed that if a man married a widow other than by a smock wedding he took over the debts of her former husband. To avoid this, she came to him naked, thus demonstrating that she brought nothing with her from her previous life. Decency had to be preserved, however, so she came to church dressed in a sheet or a smock, purchased by the bridegroom. The most recent Wiltshire example which I have been able to find occurred at Chitterne All Saints on 17 October 1714. The parish register states that on that day: 'John Bridmore and Anne Selwood were married, the aforesaid Anne Selwood was married in her smock, without any clothes or headgier on.'

14   The Weyhill Ghost

I am by no means the first writer of a book on Wiltshire to include the story of the Weyhill Ghost, although I am well aware that Weyhill is a good two miles on the Hampshire side of the Wiltshire/Hampshire boundary. Be that as it may, for centuries Weyhill Fair, held in the second week of October, was reckoned to be the greatest fair in the kingdom, attracting entries of upwards of 500,000 sheep, together with cheese, hops, horses, implements and buyers from all parts of the kingdom, including a strong contingent from Wiltshire.

The story of the Weyhill Ghost first appeared in the *Boston Gazette* around the year 1811 and has since been repeated a number of times. It concerns a man named Leadbetter, a hop merchant, and his horrifying experience at the fair.

For many years he has made a practice of attending the great annual Fair at Weyhill, as a purchaser of that commodity in which he chiefly deals. It happened that, at the last fair, he arrived at the Inn to which he always went some hours later than usual, as travelling with a considerable sum of money for his purchases, he rarely chose to be out at night.

On going into the house he learnt, to his regret, that so much company had arrived before him that every bed was engaged; but the landlady, Mrs Symonds, proposed obtaining him a bed at the house of a neighbour. Mr

Leadbetter, however, disliked the idea of sleeping out of the Inn, and it was now too late to think of changing the arrangements of the house for the night; the gentleman therefore determined to have a bed made up on some chairs in the room where he supped.

This contrivance was about to be executed when Mrs Symonds recollected that there was an Ostler's room in the yard, which possibly Mr Leadbetter might prefer to sleeping in a room where he would be liable to be disturbed very early in the morning; and she assured her guest, if he chose to sleep there, the linen should be clean, although the appearance of the room was not elegant, and the Ostler would sleep in the stable or go out somewhere.

To this the gentleman willingly acceded; and, after some short time, he passed up the gallery in the yard which led to it and retired to bed.

Sleep lent its leaden influence soon to the weary traveller, and he enjoyed soundly the sweet oblivion of anxiety – until a strange noise in the gallery which he had ascended roused him into sense again. The noise was that of an extremely heavy footstep.

Mr Leadbetter counted every step, and to his alarm the sound increased until the cause of it reached the door of his apartment. In an instant a tall, gaunt figure entered the room with a candle in one hand and a butcher's knife in the other!

Mr Leadbetter attempted to speak, but his voice failed him – and the figure approached the bed! It seized and shook the horror-stricken man; then drew the knife several times across its own throat. It then went to a table in the room, set down the light and immediately quitted the place, with the same awful sound that had marked its approach.

Mr Leadbetter began to breathe again. He imagined after a few minutes that he must have been dreaming, and yet the candle and candlestick on the table were no phantoms. That something had entered the room was clear. To avoid further visits of so alarming a kind Mr Leadbetter, as there was no lock or bolt on the door, determined to place something heavy against it. The room, however, was so scantily supplied with furniture that nothing but the bedstead was of any weight. As this fortunately ran on castors, the gentleman rolled it with the head to the door; and, thinking himself tolerably safe from intruders, addressed himself to sleep again.

About an hour later he heard again the same sounds which had formerly alarmed him renewed on the gallery stairs. In a few seconds the door of his room was pushed with great violence, his bed was rolled into the middle of the apartment, and again the horrid figure stood before him. The faculties of speech and motion now quite forsook him. The figure shook him again with fierce gesticulations and, again drew the knife across its throat. Mr Leadbetter saw that there were now gouts of blood on the blade which had not been there before!

The figure then passed away from the room, and Mr Leadbetter's senses fled with it. He fainted, and remained for some time insensible. At about four o'clock when he recovered he found himself lying half out of bed. With his best speed he dressed himself, descended into the yard of the inn, roused the landlord and poured out to him the story of his experiences.

Mr Symonds, on hearing the tale, was scarcely less alarmed; nor could he answer the eager enquiries of Mr Leadbetter as to where the Ostler had slept. Mr Leadbetter was satisfied that that poor man would never more be seen alive.

The house was quickly aroused, and the business of the fair was almost forgotten in the wonder excited by the story, which lost nothing by repetition to the several guests of the inn. By six o'clock the Ostler arrived from a lodging which he had got in the town, on being turned out of his usual bed. Much pleasure was expressed on seeing him, but when he had heard the story he exclaimed,

'Why, damn me! I'll lay my life I know that ghost very well. It was that deaf-and-dumb fellow that comes to help me kill the pigs. He always goes up to my room to call me when we have one to kill!'

The murder was out! It was indeed the deaf-and-dumb fellow who, thinking the Ostler lazy, had gone back a second time to call him, after he had stuck the pig. Hence Mr

Leadbetter's horror and his conviction of a bloody murder.

An Andover historian who knew the story, said that the deaf-and-dumb person was identified as 'Dummy Gale', a bricklayer by trade, who had worked at his house during his father's lifetime. The story was obviously popular, and several versions were soon in circulation. A poem or two were written about it and sold in reasonable numbers at the fair. Here is one of them:

The story spread from inn to town,
To maiden, magistrate and clown,
'Gainst every wall, 'gainst every post,
Disputes were heard about the ghost;
Thousands declared, nay thousands swore,
They'd seen the finger-marks on door,
The spot whereon the ghost had stood
With three-and-twenty drops of blood.
Such was the terror of the tale,
Each lass grew faint, each lad grew pale;
Through all the fair reigned nought but gloom;
And village beauties lost their bloom.
Look to the left, look to the right,
They dare not, fearful of the sprite;
While to decrease the people's fears,
No ghost in any play appears,
Macbeth and Hamlet, Shakespeare's boast,
Were both performed without a ghost;
In short, to tell at once the truth
Soon shut up shop, each show, each booth,
Amusements all become suspended,
And, for a time, the Fair was ended.

A word about the ceremony of 'Horning the Colts' at Weyhill Fair may not be out of place here.

At the end of the feast to celebrate the opening of the fair the landlord would call out, 'Are there any colts to be horned?'

Anyone who had not previously attended the fair was eligible. He was brought forward and seated in a chair, and on his head was placed a cap fitted with two horns. Between the horns was a cup, which was now filled with ale. The following rhyme was then recited, the whole company joining in the chorus:

Crafty is the hare; cunning is the fox;
Why should not this little calf grow up to be an ox!
To get his own living, among the briars and thorns,
And die like his daddy, with a gurt pair of horns.
  Chorus:
Horns, boys, horns; horns, boys, horns;
And die like his daddy, with a gurt pair of horns!

An alternative version would have the last line, 'And drink like his daddy, with a gurt pair of horns', but I am inclined to think that 'die' is the original and would refer to the sacrifice of the bull-god (a Celtic ritual) at the prescribed date.

The initiate then had to stand up and drink the half-gallon of ale contained in the cup, paying for another half-gallon as a forfeit if he spilled a drop (which the company ensured inevitably happened).

This ceremony was not confined to one public house; most of Weyhill's numerous inns and taverns had their own, though latterly, at any rate, The Star took pre-eminence. The set of horns used at The Star has recently come to light, after having been lost sight of for years, and is now on display in Andover Museum.

15   The Poachers

Poaching was for centuries endemic in rural Wiltshire, engaged in by half the population. Nowhere, however, was it engaged in on such a scale as in Cranborne Chase, which straddles the boundary between Wiltshire and Dorset.

In the Middle Ages the northern boundaries of the Chase were held to be somewhere along the Nadder, from Salisbury to Shaftesbury, with Harnham Bridge as a kind of frontier post. A fortnight before Midsummer Day a stag's head was mounted on the bridge. During the period when the hinds were dropping their calves, known as the Fence Month, every waggon crossing the bridge had to pay a toll of fourpence and every pack-horse a penny, as compensation for any disturbance they might have caused.

There was constant friction, but the situation was contained until James I granted the Chase to the Earl of Salisbury. The Earl tried to enforce what he understood to be ancient privileges and stirred up a hornet's nest.

The last attempt to exercise the old rights was made by Lord Rivers, who held Cranborne Chase in the early nineteenth century. With the typical arrogance of the gentry of that period he ordered farmers and estate-owners for miles around to pull down their fences, and he gave his keepers instructions to shoot all trespassing dogs. At last a court case was brought by a farmer of Alvediston, whose dog had been shot by a keeper while it was walking quietly with its master. The farmer won, and the long war was ended.

Before that, however, generations of young bloods in south Wiltshire and north Dorset found sport in conducting poaching wars in Cranborne Chase. The game was to kill deer without being caught by keepers, but if the keepers intervened, so much the better. That would mean a pitched battle, which these young hotheads enjoyed.

The young squires collected bands of retainers from the local farmers and labourers, and the keepers took to going about in groups, for protection, so sometimes considerable numbers of men were involved. Both sides evolved a kind of armour, examples of which are stored in Farnham Museum. It consisted of a long canvas coat, thickly padded with wool, and helmets of plaited straw. For weapons they had quarter-staves and short swords. The maximum fine was £30, which presented no hardship to the wealthy young landowners and farmers involved.

The situation changed in the reign of George II, when stiffer penalties were exacted. Prison was the penalty for the first offence, and anyone caught twice was transported for seven years. This had the effect of checking poaching for sport, at least for a time, but did nothing to deter the village labourers and smallholders, who poached for the pot.

Bowerchalke has a number of stories about local poachers. One concerns an old lady who, when her cottage was unexpectedly visited by keepers, saved the day by sitting on the iron pot in which the venison was cooking. A place there known as Shepherd's Cross is supposed to mark the spot where shepherds hanged for deer poaching had their bodies displayed in gibbets.

The following account, taken from a book entitled *Anecdotes and History of Cranbourn Chase*, written by William Chafin and published in 1818, is typical of what went on during the poaching war. The incident selected occurred on the Wiltshire side of the border.

Another murder, about the same time (1738) was perpetrated in Lord Pembroke's Walk, at Fernditch. One of his keepers was found dead, having been beaten in a most cruel manner with sticks or staves. One criminal alone was detected, although it was not doubted but many were accessory to the murder. This man, whose name was Wheeler, was arraigned and tried at Salisbury, found guilty and condemned to be hung in chains near the spot where the murder was committed; which sentence was duly carried out. But, in the course of a few nights after, the gibbet was cut down and the body carried away and thrown into a very deep well at some distance from the place. The weight of the irons carried it to the bottom, and it was not discovered till a long time after ...

In the year 1791 a villainous set of deer-stealers infested the Chase, particularly Rushmore Walk, and had the audacity to course and kill many deer in an inclosure (sic) close to the Lodge. Having thus been successful, the keepers suspected they would repeat their depredations. Therefore, at a particular time when the weather and other circumstances were inviting to the deer-stealers and the keepers expected them, ten of them from different lodges assembled singly in the daytime and concealed themselves in the offices of the mansion, where they remained until night approached.

The first alarm given was the crash of one of the sash windows in a room on the ground floor. One of the keepers who was nearest to the place immediately sallied forth and saw a man in the act of cutting a deer's throat, which he had just drawn from the window through which it had been forced by a dog. The keeper struck the man on the head with his staff just as he was rising from the ground. Most unfortunately the man's cap (which was made of straw, after the manner of bee-pots) gave way, and the point of the staff came into contact with the temple and killed him on the spot.

A most desperate engagement immediately ensued between the deer-stealers and the keepers, exactly equal in numbers, each party ten. The keepers were armed with staves and hangers, the enemy with swindgels. Many wounds were received and given on both sides; when the keepers, being greatly oppressed by the enemies' weapons, by gradually retreating into a plantation near the Lodge, made use of a successful finesse, for under the trees the swindgels could not be made much use of. The keepers then with their hangers made such havoc that the whole party were soon defeated. Some took to flight; others, who were badly wounded, surrendered. They were committed to the gaol at Salisbury, tried there, found guilty and transported for life.

The narrative illustrates accurately the sort of thing that went on. A swindgel, by the way, is a weapon adapted from the threshing flail.

16 The Odstock Curse

One of the most dramatic stories of old Wiltshire concerns the Odstock Curse. I came across it in the 1930s, when I was given a copy of the chronicle written by an eye-witness of most of the events, the village blacksmith of Odstock, Hiram Witt. The story seems to begin about the year 1798, and Hiram Witt wrote his account in the year 1870. Certain sequels were added to it in 1930 by his son-in-law.

The story is now widely known, particularly since I wrote a radio play around it, which was broadcast in the early 1950s. Hiram Witt's original version has, however, a dramatic quality which would be difficult to surpass and is quite remarkable from the pen of a Victorian village blacksmith. I give it here in its entirety:

> There was a time when the gipsies' children would play with the village children. There came a time when they were afraid to meet the old Queen of the Gipsies in the daytime. She was known as Mother Lee, and yet on their carts was the inscription 'Liberty Smith, Godshill, Hants'. Another inscription read 'Charity Lee, Odstock'. They had ten children, very fine and of healthy appearance. Their hair was jet black, the same as that of their parents. The old man used to oil and curl his hair, which hung several inches down his back. Especially on Sundays he dressed in a smock and Top hat, a yellow muffler around his neck. He would go to Church, and he never left the Vicarage empty-handed.

In the afternoon, the children of the villages around would pay visits to the gipsies' Camp, which was known as Joshua's Camp. It was named this in 1800. Later in this story I will explain why it was given this name.

I watched the children sit and listen to the old woman's tales, and about four o'clock in the afternoon the old woman would say,

'Now, my dears, you must go home and have your tea, and come back to school this evening and bring me a bit of tea or sugar or a bit of barley bannock or a few potatoes. You must bring something.'

There was another family, by the name of Joshua Scamp, who used the same Camp. Joshua had one son and two daughters. His oldest daughter was often seen with a young gipsy, whose name was Noah Lee, but he appeared before the magistrates and was sentenced for night poaching in Odstock Copse in the name of Noah Cooper. The magistrate asked him his proper name, and he said his mother's name was Cooper and his father's name was Joe Lee. They asked him his age also.

'About eighteen, sir,' was his reply.

Every year the farmers hired the gipsies in the spring to destroy the thistles, turnip-hoeing and to pull docks from the corn. Last of all, to cut and tie the corn, sometimes using hooks and sometimes scythes. When the harvest was ended, they were paid their Harvest Money and had a nice supper and a very lively time afterwards. Plenty of cider and home-brewed ale was consumed. Old Gypsy Lee would play the old Fiddle, and his daughter the Tamboreen. The same instruments they used at their Fatal Wedding, which I will come to later.

The day after the Harvest Supper they would pack up. One half went to Farnborough and the other half to Kent, picking hops. They always returned to Salisbury Fair, about the middle of October. They were fairly rich when they came back. They visited the old beer house and spent a good bit of their Harvest Money. If they took their children the landlord would not allow them inside, so the gipsies brought their own mugs and basins and were served through the windows. The beer house is called the Yew Tree

Inn, and the landlord's name is Bracher ...

I have already told you Joshua's daughter was often seen with Gypsy Lee, the man with two names. Eventually they got married. Several of the villagers were invited to the wedding – the carpenter, the blacksmith and the sexton as well. On many occasions in the old public house they laughed and talked about this ceremony.

The bride and bridegroom take each other's hands. The fathers-in-law, they cross hands – Joshua Scamp, the bride's father, and Joseph Lee, the bridegroom's father. It is decided before the clock strikes twelve that they are man and wife as long as they live. They were eating and drinking, playing and dancing, until twelve o'clock around a large camp fire in the old Clump. The newly-married couple went to the Chalk Pit, where a new tent had been erected for the occasion.

They had been married about five months when Old Mother Lee missed some of her tinware, which she used to hawk from door to door. She told the blacksmith she would put evil luck on the person that stole it. She asked him to lend her a looking-glass, which he did. Then she remarked, 'I shall find the thief and my lost tinware.'

Which she did, at Noah Lee's Camp in the Chalk Pit.

Noah worked the villages with ware, potato nets and clothes' pegs. He owned some good dogs, ferrets and nets. He was warned off all the camps on the Earl of Radnor's estate.

He went to the New Forest gypsies' camp near Godshill. He came to Odstock to see his father-in-law, Joshua, one Sunday, and he stole the old man's velveteen coat with large brass buttons on it. Joshua had bought this coat in Salisbury.

Noah told his wife one evening he was going to Southampton, but he took his pony, taking Joshua's coat to ride on, and went to South Newton instead, a few miles out of Salisbury. He arrived at the Beer House there and enquired the way to Warminster. He returned to his wife two days later and took her to Romsey.

Old Joshua missed his coat but blamed another camp follower by the name of Jack Bachelor. There were two brothers, the other named Bob. They were very much alike, and they were not guilty of doing any man out of a hard day's work. They were big men – over six foot in height. They were from thirty to thirty-five years of age. They would fight or wrestle, were good at single-sticks and have won a good many cheap drinks at any of these games. They had a good many meals and shelter in Joshua's tent.

Jack Bachelor was questioned by Joshua about the missing coat, but that was a serious mistake and caused a free fight among the gipsies. There was not any gypsy who could beat the Bachelors at that Camp, but later on in the week two men came from Idmiston Camp. Their names were Jack Bull and Nelson Lee. A fight was arranged and took place in the Chalk Pit. Many of the villagers witnessed it.

Just a pair of trousers only they were wearing. Bull was the winner against Bob Bachelor. Then came Nelson Lee against Jack Bachelor. Nelson was winning, but Bob Bachelor intervened and struck him unconscious. The gypsies shouted, 'Two to one isn't fair!' There was a heap of stones nearby, and the gypsies old and young pelted the brothers till they begged for mercy. They were a little quieter after this, but neither of the Bachelors was allowed in the Odstock Camps. The villagers, even to the little children, were glad to know that the big bully brothers had been taken down a notch, but that was not the end of it. It was years afterwards that they had their last fight.

We now go back to Joshua and the coat. Joshua was a better-class gypsy – very quiet, especially after the death of his wife. It is a pity his daughter had not died instead.

The gypsy children used to come to the Forge. I must tell you about these children. The blacksmith had a pair of tongs, with round, flat jaws. He would get them hot. The gypsies would bring a quantity of barley and wheat meal and mix it with water. Sometimes the blacksmith would give them a few currants and a bit of sugar. They put a tablespoonful of dough between these tongs. The blacksmith squeezed the handles together, holding them for a few seconds, open the tongs and out fell the biscuits, ready cooked. They called them Pat-a-cakes. The blacksmith often felt sorry that he had showed them how to make these cakes, as they often worried him when he was very busy.

We come to the morning when Joshua's second daughter, eighteen years old, was at the Forge waiting for her donkey to be shod. The old donkey was nearly finished when a strange man came to the smithy. He was a pedlar, selling boot-laces, and he also had a few rabbit-skins on his back. Joshua's daughter looked at him very hard when he was leaving the shop. She spoke her father's death sentence. She said, 'Father, that man is wearing the coat that you lost.'

Old Joshua was sharpening his knife on the grinding-stone. He asked the man, 'How did you come by that coat?'

The answer was, 'I got it from a man in Salisbury. I can shew you the man if you will come to Salisbury with me.'

Joshua, thinking that this would be Bachelor, the thief, went with the donkey and cart, the pedlar walking at his side. He asked Joshua to let his daughter come as well, as a witness.

When they got to Salisbury he told Joshua he would report the matter to the super of the Police Force. When they entered the Police Station he told the super that Joshua owned the coat. The super asked Joshua whether he was certain that it was his property.

'Yes, sir, I can tell you how certain marks came here and there.'

'Then I must make you a prisoner.'

Joshua was charged with stealing a valuable cart horse at South Newton. Poor Nellie took the donkey and cart home but left her father behind. She had not been wanted as a witness; she was wanted to bring back the donkey. The Pedlar was a Policeman in disguise.

The night the horse had been stolen Joshua had not left the Camp. When the trial came on there were several witnesses who swore on oath that Joshua was in Camp at ten p.m., and that a man with a pony and cart-horse were seen at Wilton at 10.30, and that it was impossible for any man to go eleven miles in half-an-hour. Joshua's coat had been left in the stable at South Newton. But the truth came to light when it was too late. People never believed that Joshua was guilty, and the village seemed doomed for years afterwards.

The case lasted but three hours. Joshua was sentenced to

death and hanged in public, and I amongst thousands will never forget the terrible scene.

The name of the Governor of the Prison was Dowding. The coffin was made at Odstock by a carpenter by the name of Bracher. Joshua saw his coffin and said it would do.

When he was on the scaffold he asked for the cap to be removed. This was granted, as he wished to see his friends once more. It was awful to see and hear the screams and shoutings. There was fighting all the way down Fisherton Street to the Market Square in Salisbury. All the beer houses were closed for several hours.

At Odstock that night there was a dim light in poor old Joshua's Camp. The grave was dug at the south side of Odstock churchyard. There were hundreds of people at the funeral. The gypsies disappeared very quietly next day. Joshua's younger daughter, Nellie, and her brother Tom went to Woodgreen Camp. The old Queen of the Gypsies was in hospital with a fractured leg at the time.

Joshua's son-in-law Noah was not at the execution or the funeral. The same year saw a considerable lot of horse and sheep stealing going on. Sheep and deer were often rushed to Whiteparish Hill, and a Southampton man would be there to receive the bootleg.

One Sunday morning a chestnut hunter was missing from a farm near the New Forest. This horse was traced to a place about three miles from Winchester. There were several horses turned out in a pasture for the season, and several chestnuts among them. The stolen horse had a long tail and a silver mane, which had been cut off. However, when the owner went to the pasture and called to his mare, of course she came, although he was sixty yards away. They left her there but kept a sharp look-out.

A man was seen driving by daily and looking very hard at the horses. This man resided at Brook Street, Winchester. They got to know where he lived and the beer house he used. Two men went into the beer house one Sunday evening. Each of them had a horse whip. They got into conversation with the man and treated him to a quantity of beer. They were supposed to be horse-dealers who were going to Reading that night. They had plenty of money and, flashing a hand full of gold, said they were prepared to buy twenty horses and pay for them at the same time. The man asked how much they would give for a hunter five years old.

'We must see it first.'

He said, 'Yes. Come with me.'

They were soon on their way through Kingsworthy. One man stayed with the pony; the other caught the Hunter. They were all back in Winchester by half-past nine.

'How much do you want for the Hunter?'

'Twenty pounds.'

'How did you get this mare?'

The answer was not very satisfactory.

'What is your name?'

'Noah Lee.'

'Yes, we know. We are Police Constables, and we intend to charge you with stealing this horse.'

He was wanted for theft in another county as well, and for stealing two ponies. The trial came on. He was found guilty and hanged.

His wife had a baby at the time, and she told the Police everything concerning her Father's death. The curse of the old Gypsy Queen who had cursed them for stealing her tinware had come true. She said that when she had visited her Father in the condemned cell he had taken her hand and said,

'Mary, I am seventy-one years old and my time is short. Your husband, Noah, is not yet twenty-one and he may have a long life before him, but he must be very careful. I believe he stole my coat and left it at South Newton.'

She used to say,

'If my Father had told me to divulge the secret I would have done so, but he begged me not to do so. The night that Noah went out and told me he would not return till the morning he did take my Father's coat, and a halter for the horse. The day my Father was executed we stayed in the New Forest. I told Noah he would have to suffer for it some day or other.'

When the people of the towns and villages heard of Noah's arrest and sentence they were not at all surprised. Not only gypsies but other people visited the grave of Joshua at

Odstock. Various cards and flowers were placed on the grave.

Everyone seemed to sympathize with Joshua's children. Mary often visited Odstock and never went away hungry or penniless. The baby died shortly afterwards and was buried at Odstock. It was a blessing, too. Her brother Tom and siser Nellie went up near Lyndhurst and lived together. They came to visit their Father's grave the Sunday after a very nice headstone had been erected.

The terrible happenings which I now relate occurred some few years afterwards. Some people thought the Vicar and Churchwardens were to blame.

On the anniversary of the funeral the gypsies arrived at Joshua's Camp. On the Saturday previous old Bracher at the Yew Tree Inn would get in an extra stock of beer and cider for them. Flowers of all descriptions were put on his grave on the Sunday morning. They also planted thorns and briars around his grave and a small yew tree at the foot of the grave.

The yew tree grew rapidly and became unsightly. The Vicar informed the gypsies they were to pull it down. This they would not do. So the Easter vestry decided that it had to pull it all up, and this was done by the old Sexton. His name was Hackett. The Vicar's name was Groves. The Churchwarden's name was Hodding, who was a farmer of a thousand acres in Odstock. There is a tableau for all of them in the church.

The son and daughter of Joshua Scamp visited the grave and saw what had happened. The news was soon circulated to the various gypsy camps.

The gypsies arrived in scores on a Sunday morning. The old Queen led the army of Romanies to the Churchyard. They were greatly annoyed. They entered the Church and destroyed everything they could find. There were several yew trees in the Churchyard, and they pulled up every one. They cut the bell rope. There was no service that morning. The shouting and cursing were awful.

They went to the Beer House, and Mr Bracher did a wise thing. He upheld their actions; otherwise it would have been a bad thing for him. They sat on the walls and banks and ate and drank till everything was gone. They had plenty of food and drink given them. Among them were the two brothers named Bachelor.

The old King and Queen stood on the gate by the Church and swore what they would do. The old woman removed her bonnet. She put one hand over her eyes and pronounced five curses of bad luck. The first was on the Parson. She took her hands from her eyes and clenched both her fists.

'You will not be preaching this time next year.'

To Mr Hodding the farmer she said with a scream, 'Bad luck will follow you. No son of yours shall ever farm your land.'

To the Sexton she shouted, 'You shall be found dead before twelve months more.'

That same evening twenty-five special Police Constables were sworn in. They were each armed with a club stick, and their pay was two shillings and sixpence. Some of them were set to gather small quickthorns and various small shrubs to plant on the grave. When they met at the church gate, prominent among them were the Bachelor brothers. They had turned traitor against the tribes who had befriended them on so many occasions.

In the morning in the church the old Queen happened to drop her shawl. She went along next day to find it and was given it back again. Several constables were still there. One of them gave her a push and locked the church door behind her. This annoyed her very much. She shouted another curse.

'Any person who hereafter locks this door will die before the year is out.'

Then she saw the Bachelor brothers and went into a terrible rage. Clenching her fist she said, 'You will die together, and very quickly.'

You could hear her screeching in the next village, Nunton.

The gypsies cleared out of their camps in the next few days. Before they left the King and Queen put a bunch of flowers on Joshua's grave. They also planted geraniums there, given them by a shepherd at Odstock. Before they left the Queen told Mr Witt, the old blacksmith, 'My wishes will come true before I come here again.'

As the spring came once more, the farmers were not allowed to hire any gypsy. Farmer Hodding did not want to. His heart was broken, and he regretted ever attending that Vestry meeting. He did get bad luck for the next two seasons. First, his valuable dairy herd of young and middle-aged animals were struck down with anthrax. They were slaughtered and burnt in the pasture near the Avenue. I saw the constable watching them burn day and night for several weeks. The following year his lambs died by the score. Nearly everyone you met remarked about how the Gypsy's curse was working out.

Then came the curse of the Parson. He was stricken ill with a bad throat. He had an impediment in his speech, so that you could not understand what he said. Soon he died.

John Hackett, the sexton, was found dead by the side of the road one morning, before he reached his work in Longford Park.

As the Bachelor brothers had enrolled as Special Constables they were allowed to do a bit of farm work. A party of five men came for the harvesting. They became friendly with the Bachelors. Their camp was on the Shoulder of Mutton Down, and they would always go into Salisbury on Saturdays and reach the beer house at Odstock at nine or ten o'clock. One Saturday night the Bachelors got to the beer house an hour before the other men and later went off towards the camp. They were seen by the keeper, whose name was Tillford. Each carried a rush basket. Some of the gypsies had a camp close by, where they had a nice fire. Early in the morning the keeper moved them on, but the Bachelors were never seen again. Nobody ever troubled about them, as they were so undesirable and they had overdrawn their harvest money, but it seems queer that the keeper saw a rush basket partly burned when he kicked the fire out. They never came back to harvest.

That was nine years ago (1861). We have a new vicar, farmer and sexton in the village. I often pay a visit to Joshua's grave, as my father and brother are buried close to him. My brother saw the execution, and I was there too. I asked my father to lift me up in his arms, as I could not see ...

At this point Hiram Witt's narrative ends, but the story of the Odstock Curse does not. Local people have told me that Hiram did not record the full details about Farmer Hodding. After the curse, his wife bore him several sons, all of whom were born dead. A broken man, Farmer Hodding sold up and emigrated to Australia.

About 1924 the Downs above Odstock were taken over to be converted into a racing establishment and were cleared to make gallops. One day in 1929 the manager noticed some uneven spots in the turf. Digging, he found two skeletons, side by side. Mr Feltham, Hiram Witt's son-in-law, recorded:

> They were exactly the same size and length. They measured six foot six. The bones were in good preservation, the jawbones sound, the teeth white. The bones were sent to Birmingham to Sir Charles Hyde but were returned and reburied in the place where they were found. The old saying 'What is done in the dark shall come to the light' is true ...

Local folk were convinced that these were the bones of the Bachelor brothers. They remembered the curse, that the brothers should die quickly and together, and that they should not live to see another harvest.

There remains the curse on the church door. It too has worked out dramatically. About the year 1900 an Odstock carpenter was employed to make a pair of new gates for the churchyard. One of his contemporaries takes up the story:

> While he was working on the gates the sexton brought up the subject of locking the church door, which had not been locked since the Curse. The carpenter laughed that the Curse was all rubbish and that he was not afraid to lock it. The sexton advised him not to, if he wanted to live

another year, but his mind was made up. It was a job to move the bolt, after all those years, but the carpenter managed it eventually.

This was spring-time. The sexton, half-jocularly, used to say, 'Well, only so many months to Christmas and the end of the year ...'

One morning he heard groaning from the carpenter's cottage. The sexton and the parson broke down the door and found the carpenter very ill in bed. The doctor sent him to hospital.

When we visited him a fortnight later he said he was nearly ready to come home. But the doctor said there was not much he could do for him and sent him to another hospital in Bournemouth. He was there for nearly three weeks. His dinner was handed to him and he remarked, 'I shall get so fat in here my people will not know me when I get home.'

But he never ate that dinner. He died suddenly. His coffin was made on the same premises as Joshua Scamp's. He was buried beween the gates he had made and the church door ...

In the 1930s the then rector of Odstock had to go abroad for six months for his health. In his absence his locum, laughing at the nonsense of the curse, locked the church door. He died within a year.

The rector, when he returned, threw the key into the River Ebble. The church door is never locked.

When last I visited Odstock churchyard a briar rose was twining itself around Joshua's tombstone. A radio play I wrote about the curse attracted much attention locally and apparently resulted in a considerable augmentation of the Odstock church congregation for a few Sundays! An old lady from an old people's home in Salisbury walked the two miles over the Downs to put a posy of flowers on Joshua's grave.

'I think he deserved it,' she said. 'Don't you?'

And still the curse has not exhausted itself. Or has it?

In 1990 a young man decided he knew where to look for the key. He had studied the stream and made up his mind where the rector must have stood when he threw it in the water. So he took a few days off work and set about dredging in the mud at the bottom of the little stream.

He had spent only a few days there when on his way home he had an accident with his motor-cycle and was killed.

'Did he find the key?'

'Nobody knows,' was the answer.

But there are superstitious people who suspect the curse is still working.

Afterthought

One delightful story forms a pleasant contrast to some of the more sinister and gruesome spectres recorded in this book.

Phillips' House at Dinton is a fine country mansion now used for educational courses by several organizations, and I have often lectured there. Once the home of the Wyndham family, today it belongs to the National Trust. A feature of the building is the impressive staircase with balustrade, descending to a spacious hall. Not long ago a lady attending a course came out of her bedroom at about midnight and saw the elegant figure of a lady in filmy clothes descending the staircase. The next day she naturally told her story, and with her companions she watched for the ghost on subsequent nights, without success.

At the social evening on the final night of the course another member of the group confessed:

I hope you will forgive me but that magnificent stairway fascinated me. I thought of Regency ladies floating down the steps on their way to a ball, with the horse and carriage waiting outside. What a wonderful feeling it must have been, I thought! So I just had to try it for myself. That night I put on my prettiest nightdress and a floral dressing-gown, and when I thought that everyone was asleep I walked down the stairs to my imaginary carriage! I didn't know that anyone had seen me.